# STELLAR
### uplevel in love and reach your full potential through nature connection

## A self-help book about cultivating self-love through nature connection

Tammy L Schmidt
**Fleurbain Publishing**

Cover design: Tammy L. Schmidt


Cataloguing data available from Library and Archives Canada
ISBN: 978-1-0689402-0-0


Printed on demand by Kindle Direct Publishing, a division of Amazon.  Environmental consciousness is important to Amazon. As a manufacture-on-demand company, they produce units as they're ordered, which reduces excess production. They also maintain a commitment to recycling waste materials resulting from the printing process and from daily office operations, and they will continue to review their practices to ensure they are doing our part to protect the environment.

Fleurbain Publishing

To you, dear Rosebud, Erin, and Julep.
You are stars.

# Contents

# Introduction

You are a Star
You are outstanding, wonderful, and better than you believe — you are stellar.
Stellar is from the Latin word stella, meaning star.
You are a star.
You are meant to shine with all you've got.
It makes no sense that you would ever have to dim yourself so someone else can shine bright.
It is crazy to think that you, the star, would ever live to bask in the light of another.
The brighter you shine, the better.
Bright stars play strong roles in their constellations.
There is no reason to not shine as bright as you can.
We are all stars; we are all meant to shine.

## To Shine Again

When you are codependent, you are habitually focused on that which is beyond yourself. It can be a partner, it can be a substance, such as alcohol, or activity, such as obsessive scrolling on social media. As couples therapist Alicia Muñoz aptly puts it, "...you can become like a ship that's all sails with no anchor. You float around on the currents and breezes of others' needs, requests, desires, and schedules—adrift, at best; at worst, lost."

It might be obvious, but losing yourself in your personal relationships, substances, and activities can impede you from living to your full potential. Early learned self-limiting behaviors, commonly expected from women and girls, and survival techniques that were once so helpful to you for coping with adversity can outgrow their usefulness, and even become maladaptive when coping with trauma and its aftereffects. The habit of worrying about others more than yourself can creep up and crowd out your personal ambitions. Simply put, if you are in the habit of constantly focusing on others, you are neglecting yourself. This habit steals your fire, and you shine less bright in your life.

To shine is a metaphor for feeling your best. It means you have a strong sense of who you are. You love yourself, and you can show up in your world as a positive and productive person. You are your authentic self.

In healthy relationships, there is equal give and take. Codependency is a dysfunctional relationship dynamic where one person acts as the giver and the other person is the taker. If you are codependent, you have a baked-in self-limiting tendency to forget yourself and focus on the lives and interests of others. You may fear rejection and avoid conflict so you can maintain the approval of others. You may have difficulty being alone. And because you are afraid of being alone, you may fearfully try to control that which you don't want to lose. You may enable harmful behaviour, such as addictions, exhibited by your loved ones. If you are struggling with codependency, you have lost sight of who you are, and you rely on external sources to define who you are. It can be very difficult for you to set healthy boundaries. These behaviors can be a magnet for narcissists and other self-absorbed people, or businesses, such as social media companies, competing with their algorithms designed to monopolize a steady supply of attention.

Until you focus your energy, your light, back on yourself with regular self-care practices, you will not be able to shine like the star you were born to be.

Trauma and limiting beliefs restrict your ability to shine. Trauma can result from missing something you should have received, or it can be from experiencing something you should not have experienced. Trauma is an experience that is energetically lodged in the body. You have a hard time letting it go. Like having the radio playing annoying music all day, trauma becomes an ever-present preoccupation that can distract your thinking and actions until you make a serious commitment to changing the station. You can help yourself by taking action such as seeing a therapist and a life coach, listening to calming guided meditations, gratitude and daily affirmations, taking care of your body, and getting involved in your community. Limiting beliefs can originate from what teachers and caregivers teach you in childhood. They can also be reinforced through negative experiences any time throughout life. Women and girls are taught to focus on others, to not rock the boat, and to be people-pleasers. The distorted teachings we received create limiting beliefs and keep women from being their best, happiest self.

I have developed the Stellar method of nature connection to support the work of taking small, daily steps away from trauma and limiting beliefs towards a greater love of self and an authentic life. It is from here where you can shine bright. Nature connection offers a counterbalance for people caught in the habit of putting more focus on others than themselves.

Taking those steps out the door and into a greenspace are steps back to yourself each day. Recovering from codependency requires that you make your way back to self-acceptance and self-love. It shifts your attention from anything outside of yourself, to shining your light on yourself, in an expansive way, into the realm of the here and now. It is a habit that allows you to reorganize your mind and your day to reflect what is most important to you. You become the caretaker for your own emotional well-being. Overcoming codependency requires a focused commitment to yourself, but in the end it is worth it. In the end you will find you best, most authentic self.

## What You Can Expect from The Stellar Method of Nature Connection

I wrote this book for you, a person who longs to shine in your life, and yet despite your best efforts you're confronting stumbling blocks and finding it harder than you'd thought it would be to feel like you can thrive and shine. You may struggle with trauma or limiting beliefs. You may be recovering from codependent patterns in relationships, with social media, or have struggled with self-concept and learned selflessness making you vulnerable to self-interested people. I wrote this book for you if you over-give in your personal relationships. This is for you if you are ready to make positive shifts in your life and you are open to stress-relieving practices fostering self-acceptance, happiness, peace and joy. My writing is based upon my own journey of recovery, and discovery. I would love to say that I wrote this book thinking these challenges mostly affect women, but in my experience, men can fall victim to such relationship dynamics as well.

Each time I make bold moves to interrupt patterns reflecting my trauma or limiting beliefs, and commit to self-care, I end up in better alignment with who I am, and I receive more of what I want. Yes, sometimes this creates a dramatic and unexpected shake-up in my life.

It sometimes means being the one who has to leave, uprooting yourself, sometimes ending relationships, like friendships and romantic partnerships that have become detrimental to your sense of wellbeing. It can mean accepting that when you take care of your needs, people who are used to you always putting them first aren't going to like it. Standing up for yourself can rub people the wrong way when they're used to you always putting them first and never looking out for yourself. Change can be hard. Sometimes it can sting. But after the shake up, life improves. I end up finding opportunities that reflect more of what I actually want and need. Life improves and I'm a healthier, happier, freer me.

## Living in alignment requires you to show up for yourself first.

Spending time in nature is an easy-to-do, no equipment required, self-care practice that helps maintain both physical and mental health. If you struggle with making yourself the star of your life, the Stellar method of nature connection can help. It is a practice that allows you to know yourself better. You take time to feel your feelings and emotions, and name them. You tune into your intuition and gain information about your life. You ground and center, allowing your body to relax. You offer gratitude and affirm that you are connected to more than yourself. In general, this practice will help you overcome challenges with your best energy and improve your ability to show up in your life. You will be more relaxed and less stressed, you will be happier, more joyful, and inspired. You can expect more freedom from self-limiting patterns, better relationships, more time for the things that really matter to you. This means that you can expect to live a more fulfilling and authentic life. You can expect to feel better about yourself and improve the capacity to love yourself.

## Back to the Woods

I'm a nature lover who works as a professional nature therapy guide and an experiential herbalist. I have dedicated most of my adult life to the study and use of herbal medicine. In my pursuit to understand this domain sufficiently, I studied to become a Clinical Herbal Therapist through Dominion Herbal College. This is a vast and exciting area that I will never stop exploring.

In college, I learned how to use herbs at a specific dosage to elicit a healing response in the body. Some herbs, like the ones we use in food or as a nourishing infusion, such as stinging nettles, are adaptable and can be used at various dosages. Other herbs, like lobelia, commonly called puke weed, require caution and they must be used in precise dosages. I bet you can guess what happens when you take too much puke weed! Combining my experience as a Clinical Herbal Therapist and a nature therapy guide, I was curious about the healing that happens on a global level simply by immersing myself in nature.

In my experience over the last few years, I have realized that there is a new type of infusion to consider when considering plant medicine. It requires no precise dosage and no specialized measuring equipment to bring about healthful results. We can infuse ourselves in the forest. It may seem like a funny idea at first, but spending time in nature is a global approach to health that can gently and visibly improve many systems of the body at once. Notably, anything related to too much stress can be improved through nature connection. Immersing yourself in nature is complementary to allopathic medicine and other healing modalities.

Becoming a nature therapy guide through the Association of Nature and Forest Therapy (ANFT) in 2020 has been an influence and grounded me in training, but it is the daily practice of visiting natural spaces such as forests, gardens and city parks where I have gained my best experience. My daily practice helped me improve my physical and mental health.

In March of 2020, all our lives changed forever when the COVID-19 pandemic hit. At that point in time, I was a freshly minted Nature and Forest Therapy Guide, and it became abundantly clear that nature connection was a great way to help me reduce anxiety and stay calm when my stress levels ran high. As I recall, (and you do too, I'm sure), each day was full of uncertainty. Visiting a forest or green space was something tangible I could do to help myself during a time when all of us were unsure of the future.

At the time, there was an ever-present apprehension in the air. Each day, I woke up and I waited to hear what would happen next, where we were at, and what to do. Watching the news or reading people's extremely panicked posts, especially the stay the f*ck home ones on Facebook, sent my anxiety levels through the roof. Taking a walk to the forest calmed me down and brought everything back into perspective.

I'd already trained with the ANFT, but during the pandemic I began to truly understand the importance of nature connection in a new way. The daily practice of nature connection became an obvious necessity– only a few weeks into the pandemic. No matter what challenges played out around me, and how they made me feel, if I bundled up and went outside, nature connection grounded me, brought me calm and helped me stay centered. After returning to greenspaces day after day, I noticed that from this calm and centered place, I could make better decisions, and my intuition became stronger. It helped me stay in tune with what felt best. And this remembering of what felt best, the most calm and positive, reminded me that I like to feel my very best as much as possible. I ended up taking less crap from others, to put it bluntly, and I focused on what mattered to me.

Aside from working as an herbalist and nature therapy guide, I have studied energy medicine with Denise Linn and Meadow Linn, and Cyndi Dale. I have coaching training from the Wayfinder Coaching Program with Martha Beck. And going way back, in my early years I was a minister working as an educator and community organizer.

## Overview of the Content

In this book you will discover:

• Some of the studied benefits from spending time in nature.

• The difference between spending time in nature and a nature connection.

• How self-love can help us, our communities, and the planet.

• The seven steps of the Stellar method of nature connection.

• How to check in with your emotions each day and empower yourself to feel your best.

• How gratitude reminds you that you are connected to Source.

• How to access your greater knowing through intuition.

• How nature connection supports making good decisions and living courageously.

• What it means to be in a healthy interdependent relationship

• Inspiration to keep going with nature connection, especially during the tough times and transition.

• A link to a guide to use in the Stellar method nature connection.

## The Lessons in Sweet Solitude

Throughout my life, I'm proud to say that I've been aware and always growing. Healing isn't a linear process, but throughout my life I continued to put the pieces together. This last year has been one of the most exceptional times in my life. By circumstance and by deliberate choice, I am at the one-year mark of almost total isolation. I made time and space for growth and realignment as I heal from past relationships and childhood trauma. Along with participating in coaching programs, and reading self-help books, I have faced myself, and offered myself time for deep introspection to explore the origins of my self-limiting patterns.

Over the course of a year, I have lived how I want, not only that but I have provided all my own needs, including building fires each night through the winter. I have always known that I am independent, but I have experienced my own strength and ability to care for myself and all my needs. I have learned that I am very good at organizing a healthy lifestyle for myself. I have a kick-butt daily workout routine and I eat only the foods I love and healthy foods most of the time. I wear clothes that make me feel good. I've lost weight without any mad restrictions. I celebrate holidays the way I want. Self-care is woven throughout my life: I listen to fun music, I read books, I garden, I take long baths, and go outside to nature connect whenever I want to. I have faced my tendency to procrastinate with my professional projects and I have established a work routine doing work I love. I feel good about my work as it makes a positive contribution to the world. Most importantly,

I have become my own best friend. I know how to face and move through difficult emotions. I am more relaxed and happier and I have a renewed body confidence, and I feel good in my body. I am not lonely: time alone is a sweet solitude I love.

During this special stretch of my life, I have explored the self-limiting roles I allowed for myself as an adult. I say allow because I always believe we have choices. Yes, there are forces working against us being our vibrant selves, but it is always our choice how we will perceive it and what we will do with it. Yes, ancestral limiting patterns are passed down the generations, but we can always choose to do it differently. Also, imagination is huge in creating your life. What part of me was imagining so many limits?

## The Use of Archetypes in This Book

An archetype can be defined as a very typical example of a person. Archetypes are the main characters for the short stories throughout this book. They illustrate how the Stellar method of nature connection can create change in your life. Can you see how you have embodied several archetypes throughout your lifetime? There were many factors in creating the archetype you were embodying, such as age, environment, self-concept, projects, and worldview. It's helpful to explore the role you play in your relationships and to imagine yourself as an archetype. When looking at past relationships, you can see that you were playing a part. You don't have to play that part anymore; you get to be a new character. In this way, past trauma and victimhood don't need to define you. It may be part of your story, but you don't need to let it be the whole story. You're way too fine for that!

The best way out of the story where you are the victim is to stop being a victim. Be empathetic and help yourself out of it.

It takes time, that's why practices like daily nature connections can be so helpful. It's a sustained practice that you can implement each day and continue until you feel better. In addition to personal habits such as nature connection, seek help. It is a deep form of self-care to receive support in your positive changes. Change your mindset, your surroundings, your network. Remove yourself from the problem so you can thrive. You have it in you to embody new and positive archetypes. Add to your story with new and empowering experiences and you will no longer be a victim.

Repeating patterns deserve another look. It deserves an awareness of all the parts, the stories, the little things that snagged you, the big things that crushed you. It deserves deep introspection. You need to know who's on the bus and not let any of them drive the bus. Your life, your actions deserve more than that. You want to be aware and decide how this bus rolls down the road. Until you know who is on the bus, you run the risk of these traumas driving the bus. Yeah, I am referring to you as a bus, a bit weird, but at least you have a good view of who is on board. You want to know what you are carrying so you can figure out the next steps in dealing with it.

Nature connection using the Stellar method as I have out-lined in this book, allows for daily emotional check-ins and tune-ups. It helps you know what you are carrying each day, emotionally, and empowers you to change it as you wish. Building on the nature connection practice I initiated during the COVID 19 pandemic, I have developed the Stellar method as a form of dynamic and adaptable self-care. After a few years of practice, I discovered that it is my medicine. As I worked to get to the root of my challenges in limiting behaviors and self-sabotaging tendencies, I was able to see why nature connection is magic. The Stellar method was developed for people like me, including empaths, with a history of codepen-dency, and those who have had challenges to maintain secure attachments with others. Anyone looking for a healthy self-care practice, one that complements therapy, I suggest you check this out.

No matter what is happening in the world or in your personal life, you can access stress relief and improve your outlook on life through the self-care practice of nature connection.

In the winter of 2021, I finally connected the dots and realized that daily nature connection is a relevant self-care practice that helps me cultivate self-love. Not surprising, it dawned on me as I was walking through a forest in Montreal. My experience with the daily practice of nature connection taught me that it helps sensitive and empathic people stay grounded and in tune with their inner knowing, or intuition, and supports a continuous evolution to live their best lives, creatively, courageously, and with purpose.

You will feel better with regular doses of nature connection. Not only is it necessary for physical and mental health, but it helps you ground and find your center. From this point you can show up as a better person in your life. You can rise above challenges and create a life in alignment with what you love.

The acronym STELLAR will help you reach your goals through the practice of nature connection. You are meant to shine. The more you shine, the more you can give to your work, projects, and relationships. A similar analogy for self-care is to fill your cup. Fill your cup to the brim and only give to others what you've got from the overflow. You can also imagine yourself as a star emanating light outwards. Being more of yourself and taking care of yourself allows you to shine brighter. You have it in you to illuminate the darkness. You can create strong connections with others when you shine brighter. Together with others, you help form constellations of stars. This book was created to inspire you to show up in your life with your best energy, a bright light unique to you.

If you are anything like me, eventually you want to find your way out of the mire and climb a mountain to enjoy the fresh air and expand your horizons. If you are like me, deep down you know your crap does not define you. Taking time for yourself, in a practice of self-care that is meaningful to you, can help you make your way to sunnier skies and expanded horizons. It can help you to find personal alignment to live a life where you thrive.

## Are You Ready? Let's Do This!

The method in this book is specifically for you if you are out of alignment with your true self. Something doesn't feel quite right. You are often wired and tired, a little anxious. You wish that life was more fulfilling, that you smiled more. There never seems to be enough time to do what you truly want to do. You may not make enough time for what you want or need to do to achieve your goals. You may not be able to show up in your relationships as your true self. You may tend to lose yourself in your relationships. You are afraid to move on because you don't want to lose what you've got. You wish you felt better. You may find your health is slowly declining due to not enough time for working out or eating the foods that work for you. You may treat other people better than you treat yourself. They may have lost touch with your hobbies and interests.

Even if you didn't create the problem, it is up to you to find your way to balance and healthy ways of interacting with others. You can transform your life. The power lies in you. You can take responsibility for the part you have played in relationships where you were not at your best. You are the one accepting the bad behavior of others, and you are the one who can create better boundaries and envision a life where you deserve more. You can assess the things in your life that lift you up and the things that bring you down. You can weed out what doesn't work and keep all that does. You tend your own garden and absolutely it can flourish. You can be happier. You are not stuck in the past. All your missteps didn't make anyone do or feel anything, and vice versa. You can take responsibility for your reactions, and responsibility for sometimes not knowing what was going on at the time it was happening. You can offer this from a place of compassion and forgive yourself and allow yourself to move on. You can take the steps to improve how you show up in your current relationships and have faith that you have the capacity to do better. Nature connection is an expansive practice you can offer yourself. It is something you can offer yourself daily that supports personal evolution, and it allows you to show up as your best in your life.

Do you feel tied to your pain and your recurrent thoughts from past trauma? Do you have trouble focusing on what truly matters to you? Are you overwhelmed with to-do lists for your family? Are you working hard without seeing results in your personal growth? Are you tired and wired most of the time? Does this inhibit your ability to show up in your life in the way you would want? Are you not moving forward with your life projects as you would hope? Do you feel like you are not as fit as you would like to be? Do you feel lonely and disconnected? Do you wish you were happier?

It can be difficult to look back at the challenges you have faced. The gift in surviving the challenges is the deep knowing that you are resilient, you're a survivor, and you can always figure it out. Challenges such as divorce can make you more compassionate towards others. As you face challenges, people spring up and offer their support. It's a gift to be reminded that you are not alone. Others have faced challenges, and they care to ease the burden and help you out when you are facing yours.

This book is designed to support you if you answered yes to any of the above questions. I know what it's like as I have experienced a version of this, too. Throughout my life I have diligently worked to get to the root of what has held me back.

Borrowing a concept from herbalism, the book you are reading right now was created to be a beautiful resource supporting self-care. Beautiful because beauty heals. If remedies are formulated with care and inspire positive emotions, they will work better. Sometimes the gentlest beautiful remedies, like marshmallow root and violet leaf, are the most profound because they soothe the body and allow it to relax. This ability to relax helps the body heal. Spending time in nature is a beautifully gentle way to encourage the body and mind to untangle from the events and relationships in day-to-day life. It gives you time to consider how you might best show up for yourself and respond to your world. The Stellar method is a beautiful method to support daily self-care and to create transformation in the long term.

The next 30 days you can discover the transformative power of nature connection. No matter what life throws at you, no matter what road you go down, daily self-care that allows you to feel your feelings, and decide how you are going to improve what you can will allow for sunnier days in the short term and create massive change over time. Allowing your nervous system to relax is beneficial in every way, especially when you intend to gain ground in healing entrenched limiting patterns. In as little as 17 minutes per day, you can reclaim your peace, balance and well-being. Make time for a deliberate self-care practice that delivers results and helps redirect your trajectory. Focus your actions and intentions on building an authentic life. Allow your life to blossom with nature connection and shine like a star in your life.

## How to use this book

It is recommended that people spend 120 minutes in nature each week. Does this sound like a lot? Don't worry, I've got you. 120 minutes a week is only 17 minutes a day. The method for nature connection I have created here is flexible and can be as little as a minute, with longer sessions on days when there is more time.

I challenge you to try this practice for 30 days. Reading this book and practicing nature connection for 30 days offers the opportunity to anchor the habit and create lasting change. One month offers a wide range of days, including weekdays and weekends, workdays, or getaways. In 30 days, you will encounter a range of challenges, and you will experience a wide range of feelings and emotions.

This book is structured to give you what you need to start the practice of nature connection. The information presented will help you understand the importance of nature connection as a powerful way to cultivate self-love. Where possible, the information presented is supported by scientific studies. It will motivate you to keep going and see you through the month.

# Chapter One

## Spending Time in Nature Versus Nature Connection

### We Need Time in Nature

According to the EPA, The United States Environmental Protection Agency, Americans spend 90% of their time indoors. It's hard on the body to spend this much time indoors. Doing so is correlated with an increase in insomnia, depression, attention deficit and anxiety. Most of us need more time in nature.

Spending time in greenspaces boosts your vitality by nearly 40%. Spending time indoors has the opposite effect. And why? Well, indoor spaces are often very toxic, with as much as

10 times higher levels of volatile organic compounds (VOCs) than outdoor spaces. We are surprisingly sensitive to mold, dust and pests, and noise from appliances found indoors. A lack of nature indoors can cause humans to suffer, too. Not enough fresh outdoor air can decrease the ability to focus on work. Light that does not mimic the quality of light outside messes with circadian rhythms and can lead to depression and insomnia. And not having enough nature indoors, not integrating biophilic design elements, like plants, can have a negative impact on social interaction and work performance.

There are many studies that prove we need regular doses of nature to be healthy, both physically and mentally. From The Lancet to The New York Times, to nursing research on urban forest therapy for patients, there is evidence of the healing, and the empowering elements found in regular contact with the natural world. One of the studies I drew upon to create the nature connection process outlined in this book proves that we need a minimum of 120 minutes in nature per week for physical and mental health.

120 minutes per week in greenspaces, either all at once or in short visits are "substantially more likely to report good health and psychological well-being than those who don't."

This is according to a study of 20,000 people conducted by a team led by Mathew White of the European Centre for Environment & Human Health at the University of Exeter.

There were no benefits for those who did not meet the threshold of 120 minutes. It was the same as spending no time outside.

According to the study, benefits continued to increase up to five hours per week, with no additional gain in spending more than five hours per week in nature.

The bottom-line is that it is difficult to maintain your health if you don't spend time in nature.

To achieve the necessary amount of 120 minutes in nature each week, you can make it one session of 120 minutes all at once, such as spending a Sunday afternoon in a park, or you can split the time into smaller sessions, such as 20 minutes per day.

## What We Find in Nature

Imagine yourself in a lush forest, with trees and plants all around. The air is fresh, sunlight streams through the trees, birds are singing, and you might not know why, but you feel good. All a sudden a woman arrives on the trail. She stops to greet a tree and watches the birds flying overhead. She's relaxed and smiling. It's obvious she loves this forest. When she finally notices you, she greets you with a friendly hello. You reply with a hello and shortly after remark that the air is so fresh today. She explains that the fresh scent in the air is the smell of natural chemicals called phytoncides emitted from the trees to protect the trees. These antifungal, and antibacterial phytoncides protect everything in their environment, even other plants and animals, including humans. She suggests you breathe deeply to support your immune system and the natural killer cell production in your body. It can't hurt, so you take a deep breath.

She continues to explain that the negative ions are abundant in this forest. They are generated through photosynthesis in the forest canopy, the sunlight, the water rushing by in the stream nearby, and through volatile substances released from plants. Thunderstorms also produce negative ions, but that's not happening today.

Besides reducing dust and pollution in the air, exposure to negative ions helps regulate sleep patterns, boosts mood, reduces stress, improves immune function, supports digestion, and inhibits harmful bacteria, viruses and mold. Without prompting, you take another deep breath.

There's a small plant on the forest floor that catches her attention. She finds her trowel in her satchel and digs the little plant up to use later in herbal medicine. The fresh scent of dirt wafts through the air. She explains that even the smell of dirt reduces anxiety and boosts your mood. Hmm, how wise! You take note to remember this the next time you are gardening.

She invites you to visit the forest again soon. Not only for the vitamin D produced in the body when you are in the sun, supporting immune, bone and blood health, not only for the sights and sounds that light up your senses, not only for the cooler and fresher air in the summer due to the trees acting as air conditioners and purifiers, not only since it is so peaceful and statistically there is less violence in greenspaces, but because she invites you to go mushroom picking with her. It looks like you made a friend!

## How We Benefit from Time Spent in Nature

## What are the studied mental benefits?

More and more studies are available highlighting how it is necessary for us to spend time in nature to maintain mental health.

As the biophilia hypothesis states, humans have evolved in

nature and being outside of the environment where you evolved has negative consequences. To correct this, you don't have to drop all your modern conveniences and comforts. Spending time in nature on a regular basis is enough to bring the body back to balance. It influences feelings and emotions by activating the parasympathetic nervous system which reduces stress and promotes calm.

Modern lifestyle tends to create mental fatigue that interferes with your ability to hold your attention. Being in dynamic greenspaces reduces attention deficit and improves higher order thinking and the ability to concentrate on the tasks at hand. For children, and kids at heart, being in nature provides opportunities for creativity, problem solving, discovery, risk taking, mastery and control, and supports healthy brain development.

You are more likely to feel connected when you are in nature. Of course there are plants, animals, and people. You may also feel connected to what is beyond you, such as God, the Divine or Source energy. A sense of connection reduces feelings of isolation.

Bacteria are essential in supporting life here on earth. Your microbiome is composed of bacteria, fungi, viruses, and their genes and it is found inside and on your body. These microorganisms outnumber human body cells 10 to 1! Yes, sometimes things fall out of balance and these same organisms cause illness, but often they are happily co-existing with us, supporting us. One studied example of this is the bacteria Mycobacterium vaccae. It is often found in dirt. It reduces anxiety, PTSD symptoms, fear, and improves emotional health.

Being in nature, even for a short amount of time, is like putting on your fun glasses - it increases happiness, joy, peace and optimism. It improves emotional well-being and tends to decrease rumination, which can lead to depression. The self-care practice of taking a walk outdoors in daylight, and breathing fresh air is one prevention strategy for seasonal affective disorder. It also relieves painful emotions such as worry, fear and sadness.

## What are the studied physical benefits?

Living in neighbourhoods with access to greenspaces is associated with improved well-being. Spending time in greenspaces provides "salutogenic effects on human health." Salutogenesis is the study of the origins of health and focuses on factors that support health. Check out all this evidence that nature supports your health. People who have access to greenspaces in their neighbourhoods are less likely to suffer from cardiovascular disease, obesity, diabetes, asthma hospitalization, mental distress, myopia, and premature death. People living on green streets have better quality of sleep. They have lower diastolic blood pressure, heart rate, blood cortisol, and stress. Pregnant people living near a greenspace experience better birth outcomes including birthweight. Access to a greenspace is linked to the desire to exercise more, sit less, and walk more. Interestingly, people living in cities tend to use greenspaces more than people living in the country.

Being able to view greenspaces from a hospital room reduces post-surgery hospital stays, speeds healing, and reduces the need for pain relievers.

In nature, cognitive function, thinking, and reasoning are improved. In part, this is due to natural environments inspiring soft fascination, meaning a scene that captures attention while eliciting pleasure. Urban environments force our attention to hard fascination, defined as constant stimulation, think of the constant dinging of notifications, which is very fatiguing to the body. Natural environments improve our ability to restore directed attention. This is necessary for both "executive functioning and self-regulation processes in cognition."

Greenspaces expose your body to a broad range of organisms, such as bacteria in dirt. This helps to fine tune the immune system to understand what is a threat and what is not. Reduced contact with bacteria and parasites commonly found in natural environments increases the risk of asthma, allergies, diabetes, hypersensitivities and autoimmune diseases. BVOCs or biogenic volatile organic compounds such as terpenes, essential oils, charged ions, pollen, fungi and bacteria found in large amounts in forests. BVOCs contribute to healthy immune system functioning. There are many moving pieces in this, but all in all it contributes to anti-inflammatory actions in the body. BVOCs have an anti-tumor effect in the body, both inducing tumor cell death and preventing cancers from spreading to other parts of the body. Overall, they help the body fight off cancer by aiding the increase in natural killer cells.

Practice being in nature and nature connection as much as you can as this is a salutogenic approach that is essential in supporting good health.

# Chapter Two

## Taking it Further - Turning Time in Nature into a Nature Connection.

### Time In Nature > Nature Connection

As presented above, simply being in nature offers the body so much. This book sets out to teach you how to make the most of your time in greenspaces. Nature connection is a step further than simply being in nature. It involves taking the time to slow down and sense who and what is around you. In nature connection you greet and interact with what's around you.

Simply being in nature is like walking through a crowd of people. You are immersed in the crowd but not interacting. Nature connection is like being at a concert. You are in the crowd; your senses are lit up. You are listening to the music, watching the show, perhaps interacting with the show by moving to the music along with the crowd around you. Perhaps you have drinks and snacks. You are aware of all you are sensing.

Another way to look at, being in nature is like going to a cat cafe to watch the cats around you, whereas nature connection would be interacting with the sweet cats, greeting them, basking in their glory, laughing at their funny antics, letting them lead you around the cafe, showing you their favorite toys or skills in jumping. Why do it? Because they are alive and respond positively to your actions and good intentions.

Trees and plants can respond to you as well. Nature connection is not complicated. You are already a natural. Simply slow down, sense, and remain open to find out more.

## What Is Nature Connection?

What is Nature Connection? As mentioned earlier, in the simplest terms, nature connection is slowing down and sensing nature.

Nature is defined by Oxford as the phenomena of the physical world collectively, including plants, animals, the landscape, and other features and products of the earth, as opposed to humans or human creations. Keep in mind that this includes rocks, water features, and weather patterns. Many would expand the definition of nature to include all living beings, including humans. We are nature, too.

Nature connection most often includes plants, and trees, and can include birds and insects, and animals. It may include water features such as lakes and rivers. It is often outdoors in greenspaces. In cities, we often refer to greenspace as urban vegetation or natural areas. The World Health Organization defines it as "all urban land covered by any vegetation of any kind."

## Two Points of View from May 2020

I walk up the hill to feel better,
To connect with the trees,
To notice the daily changes.
Flowers blooming
Leaves unfurling
It's the new normal- masks and distance.
Luckily, nature still invites me in.
As I walk down the hill, I spot a little bird in the grass.
Hello, little bird!
It happens again the next day. The same bird is there to greet me.
Hello, little bird!
The third time I walk down, it's there again.
It flies across the street, and I follow it.
It hops about on the tree; it shows me trees in bloom.
She introduces me to her friend. They hop on the grass.
Hello, little birds! I love seeing you here.

I notice her walking down the hill each day.
She seems to have a lot on her mind.
I see her praying and contemplating, and often in a trance with the light box she carries.
Finally, I command her attention, flitting about.
Yes, you! Hello! Nice to see you!
I hop on the grass and fly away.
Oh, look! Here she comes again!
Hello! Yes, I'm here again. Very happy to see you!

The woman looks surprised.
The next time I see her, I lead her down a new path, where the flowers are radiant on the trees. She smiles.
I introduce her to my friend. We hop about on the grass. Yes, we see you.
So happy to see you again.
Lighten up friend; there's beauty all around you.

My definition of nature connection is slowing down and being open to relating to who and what is around you in or of nature and what this may inspire in you. I keep my definition quite open because nature connection can be of value in indoor spaces, such as hospitals, workplaces, or indoors when the weather is too intense.

## Nature connection looks different each day. Examples:

• You take a walk to a greenspace, you set your timer on your phone for 15 minutes. You relax, breathe and look around you. You notice the various plants in the grass. An ant marches through the grass, the sun shines through the clouds, and a dog bounds gleefully in the distance as its owner tosses a frisbee for it to catch. A smile spontaneously appears on your face and the worry you were feeling over your pressing deadlines at work seems more manageable.

• You put on your winter gear and head outside to trudge through the snow. You slowly make your way to the greenspace, that is totally covered in snow, so it is now more of a winter-space. You set your timer on your phone for 10 minutes. You notice how your face feels versus the rest of your body bundled in layers. You notice how the fresh layer of snow makes the space so quiet. A nuthatch bird jumps about on a nearby tree. You notice that you are feeling a bit of fear and excitement over a new relationship budding after many years of being single. You take time to breathe and consider some of the exciting possibilities for the future.

• You are not feeling great, and you don't want to go outside. You make a cup of tea and sit back in your favourite comfy chair. As you sip your tea, you look out at a large maple tree in your backyard. Squirrels run back and forth on the tree. Much to your surprise a raccoon climbs the tree, and it looks like it's having a conversation with the squirrels. The whole scene makes you chuckle for a bit. The action in the tree helped you relax. For a minute, you forgot how you were feeling, and added a little levity to your day.

## How I like to define nature connection.

## Points to keep in mind:

1.  Nature connection does not need to involve movement, but it must include slowing down. Keep this in mind if you are mixing activities such as a workout, like walking or biking, or gardening and nature connection. You must slow down. You will miss a lot if you are moving quickly or if you are trying to accomplish big tasks, like gardening, while nature connecting.

2.  It doesn't require a knowledge of plants, or plant names, but it does require an awareness of what is around you and an openness to know more. You may want to be aware of what stings and bites or causes rashes. You will want to be certain about correctly identifying plants that you taste or touch. It can take a great deal of time and study to differentiate one plant from another and baby plants are famously difficult to identify. Like a guest visiting friends, it is always best to respect what is around you, remain humble in this space, and be ready to learn more.

3.   It is not a form of spirituality. It does not insist on beliefs, such as the belief that there are fairies and gnomes in the forest, though it meshes well with beliefs and spirituality.

4.   There need not be a set goal. You do not need to find beauty, to experience awe, to work through feelings, to tune into intuition, to receive information from your greater knowing, but any of the above may happen while you are nature connecting. Sometimes the very best thing to do is to allow your body and mind to simply rest and reset, without words or actions, in a peaceful space.

5.   Though it is easy to focus and calm the mind in a natural space, nature connection is not a form of meditation. The forest is an open and welcoming space for the practice of meditation, but nature connection does not need to include meditation.

6.   Nature connection involves sensing what you are sensing, what you are noticing in nature.  Run through your senses and ask yourself what you are sensing inside of you and around you. What do you see, feel, hear, smell, and even taste. The smallest details may light up for you when you do this, or you may experience a clear view of yourself within the context of life teeming around you.

7.  Nature connection is a form of self-care.  It helps prioritize the self. This type of self-care increases self-awareness and the capacity for self-love.

8.  Nature connection is complementary to many healing modalities.  It will help support an increase in positive emotions but sometimes we need more. People with clinical depression, for example, may need professional help and this primary therapy is supported with nature connection.  Another example, someone requiring medical care for a major illness will require the medical care. Healing will be supported by nature connection.

9. Nature connection is something you can do as a solo activity whereas nature therapy requires a guide.

10. Nature connection is a habit that is as important as brushing your teeth– it's best to do it every day.

11. Flexibility. I am Canadian and the weather is always a factor in how much or how little we go outside due to extreme temperatures, and cold. Though wild or natural spaces offer the most benefit, nature connection is adaptable, and it can include indoor activities such as making and enjoying cups of herbal tea, quality time with pets, caring for houseplants, visualization, formulating with herbs, creative arts including sketching, painting, morning altars or ephemeral art, dancing, writing, and taking photos.

It's important to be flexible and to include indoor nature connections. There are times in life when the weather is going sideways or, for whatever reason, we do not have access to the ideal greenspace, or urban vegetation and natural areas. We can nature connect indoors, too.

12. Nature Connection is time to focus on yourself. It's important to offer yourself nature connection as a solo activity. Solitude offers you the gift of focusing on just one person: yourself. This is not to say that you can't nature connect with people seeking to do the same; but if you do, you should also practice nature connection on your own as well.

I choose to nature connect on my own because I need time each day to anchor the habit of remaining focused on myself. For codependents, it is important that we take time to focus on ourselves. Codependent tendencies to control, support, and take care of others is a draining limitation that can be overcome. Being in nature and focusing on what is around you offers you an activity that you enjoy on your own, without friends or family. It creates a boundary in terms of your time and interests.

13. Cell Phones help enhance and support our connection to nature. I ultimately want to unplug and be present to the world around me when I am nature connecting, but I always bring my phone because they are super useful.

Cell phones have built-in timers. Use your timer to help you relax and not worry about the time. You can also take photos, notes, write journal entries, and make videos with your cell phone. It is so wonderful to take a snapshot of what happened in your nature connection. Of course, you need to manage your tech and not let it take centre stage as you nature connect, but it is a brilliant tool to bring with us in nature connection. You can also use it to contact friends to show them what surprised you in nature.

14. Meditation is easier in greenspaces. It is easier to drop-in and relax into a meditative state in nature. Part of the reason for this is that greenspaces offer an abundance of similar patterns of complexity at different scales and unperceived symmetries. These patterns are called fractals. Humans tend to enjoy seeing fractals because they increase engagement and curiosity while decreasing tension at the same time.

15. By the ways every being co-exists, nature models secure attachment style. Also, you can feel safe in nature, form healthy relationships with plants and trees, animals and spaces. This can be important when we are facing significant challenges in our relationships with humans.

16. Spending time in nature helps you develop a better sense of your intuition. Better downloads about life can happen in nature. Spending time outside of day-to-day tasks opens up the possibility of exploring who you are, your human experience, offering opportunities for self-discovery, self-care, creativity, and calm.

17. Nature is open and accessible to all. Be authentically you, nature accepts you as you are. You don't have to have status or

own anything to connect with nature. You can live anywhere and connect with nature. In my experience, urban dwellers seem to get it and value nature connection as much or more than people who live in the country. You can live in the city and nature connect.

## How to fit nature connection into your life

Nature Connection is adaptable to many environments. It is best to have many options to fulfill the recommended 20 minutes per day or 120 minutes per week.

### Go Wild

Healthy natural spaces with native plants offer the biggest benefits, but tended parks and gardens are also great. Backyards, balconies, terraces, railway corridors, back alleys are some of the typical places you will be able to easily find in cities.

### Home Body

Other forms of nature connection, in or just outside of your home include spending time with pets, making herbal tea, meditation, and visualization of being in natural spaces, looking at beautiful photographs of natural spaces and visualizing being in these spaces. Gardening can be a form of nature connection, just remember to take time to slow down. Mixing art and nature can be a form of nature connection: sketching, painting, etc., playing music, dancing or stretching, photography, writing and poetry. It can also include cooking with plants or making herbal remedies with plants. Tending plants around the house, both inside and out is a form of nature connection. What's important in all the above nature connecting is that one slows down and senses.

## Sheltering From Intense Elements

Nature connection can happen inside hospitals, greenhouses, atriums, and even your place of work. Nature connection can happen when one is stuck behind a desk at work and needs a little break. It is useful when one is ill, or for whatever reason is unable to get outside. Plants, pets, herbal tea, artwork, images on screens can all help in relaxing the body.

## Use Your Imagination

Don't underestimate the power of the imagination. It is always available. You can visualize visiting a lush rainforest, a wide prairie sky, imagining the wind, or a perfect day at the beach. And what's great about imagination is that you can be as creative as you like. You can imagine you are a bird flying there, you can teleport to the location in an instant! Visualizations aid in boosting moods and wellbeing. To visualize being in nature use your imagination to picture the scene in vivid detail. Perhaps you are hiking through the mountains, or you are visiting a Costa Rican rainforest. Include all your senses and be aware of what you would like to feel, such as joy.

# Chapter Three

Most days are busy with work and to-dos.
Let it go, even for a minute.
Take a walk in the company of trees,
let your feelings rise up and out.
The simple practice of feeling and identifying
your feelings helps to let them go.
Trees are great listeners.
They help you get to the root,
Encourage you move your limbs in the wind,
And rise to the stars.

## The STELLAR Action Plan

So far, we have talked about the difference in spending time in nature versus nature connection. Time in nature is just that. You could be doing anything, and if you are in nature you are receiving the benefit of being in nature. Nature connection involves slowing down and sensing what and who is around you. As you slow down, you give your body the opportunity to relax and recalibrate. While most of us could benefit by spending more time in nature, nature connection is adaptable to both indoors and outdoors. And this is great because some of us want to nature connect when we are stuck indoors due to bad weather, being ill, or having to work. Humans need both to spend time in nature and to nature connect to be healthy.

The STELLAR method of nature connection in this book builds on nature connection, starting with slowing down and sensing. After that, there's a 7-step framework for nature connection. It is designed for people wanting an accessible and effective self-care practice that contributes to self-awareness, grounding, and emotional regulation while helping counter the common problem of nature deficit.

## The Seven Steps

**Shed** - old energies: feel, forgive, and move on.

**Trust** - you are connected to that which is greater than you, or the Universe. Ask yourself what you are grateful for today. Practice grounding.

**Explore** - remain curious, get to know the multifaceted diamond you are, get to know the dynamic surroundings around you.

**Listen** - to your intuition.

**Live** - courageously.

**Awareness** - of ourselves in the world.

**Remain Open** - even after facing life's challenges.

## How It Works: The Flow of the Stellar Nature Connection

Take yourself to a greenspace.

Tune into the body and ask: What feeling am I feeling right now?

Make feeling state shifts in a positive direction, such as from melancholy to curiosity.

Find more expansive feeling states, such as from doubt to optimism, allow nature to inspire.

Listen to your intuition and deep inner knowing.

Make changes or take small steps in your life based on your own inner knowing, or your intuition.

Repeat.


## Another way to describe the Stellar method of nature connection

Sense what you are feeling in the moment and sensing around you while in nature. Breathe, relax, and by using your imagination, infuse your body and life with positivity.
Head back to life, centered, with positive emotions empowering your actions.  Repeat.

When you are not in tune with who you are, you have a greater tendency to lose yourself to people and projects outside the scope of what you truly want. You risk forgetting your essence, and your confidence in your authenticity. When you are not in tune with who you are, you miss out on the beautiful experience of positive change, of the metamorphosis available many times throughout life. We were born to continually evolve, as our authentic selves, almost like viewing kaleidoscope colours changing. To get the most out of life and show up as your best, you need to go inward first, have a solid connection with yourself before facing your life out there. Only you can access this inner knowing. You can't get this from others, it comes from within yourself.

The first four parts of the Stellar method happen as you nature connect. The last three parts help you to take the benefits of nature connection with you into the real world. The following sections of this book go into each step to STELLAR.

Stellar nature connection is very helpful for you if you are serious about continual evolution and making the most of your life. It helps you move beyond family norms, social norms, a station in life, and trauma. It is useful for those who want to move through this life with steady energy and confidence.

Nature connection can be a practice that helps sensitive, empathetic people (like you?) have an extra layer of regular self-reflection, ensuring you are putting the care you have for the world into the right places. It helps you make the biggest contribution as your authentic self. It helps you from being run over and taken advantage of by narcissists and others.

Spending time nature connecting allows you to tune into yourself regularly and course correct when needed. The nudges from your intuition will be stronger because you practice taking the time to listen. You do this by first going inward, before efforting and connecting out there. Nature connection in greenspaces offers the ultimate environment for this self-care habit, but it is adaptable to all spaces.

# Chapter Four

## Nature Consciousness Opens Self-Awareness

Tuning into the natural world helps you to see yourself within a larger context, thereby providing perspective on life.

I use the term nature consciousness to describe a tuning into the natural world. It is an awareness of yourself within an ecosystem and you see yourself as a part of this ecosystem. It fosters eco-awareness, or understanding of how you relate to the natural world. It causes you to look at what roles you play in ecosystems. It supports developing relationships with nature. It shifts nature connection from me to we, from what nature can do for you, provide for you, to an exploration in who we are together. From this point, nature consciousness can help provide a foundation for reflecting on your life. You are situated here, on earth, in this ecosystem, playing a role, so why not let this environment inform your decision making, and self-concept? Nature consciousness can inform you in practical ways such as how you may interact in your daily life, and what you do. It also informs you in who you are. In my experience, nourishing daily connections with nature helps me receive insights into the spiritual side of life.

Through the practice of sensing in nature, you gain experiential knowledge of what's around you, who you are, and how you are feeling. You have a choice in who you want to be in this environment and in your life. In this dynamic environment, nature consciousness can help you tune into your intuition. It helps cut through the habitual messages you tell yourself, the patterns of fear, anxiety, or other limiting beliefs. Nature consciousness can bring to life the facts of how you feel.

## We Suffer When We Don't Put Ourselves First

Falling out of alignment with our purpose can easily happen when we don't take the time to tune into ourselves on a regular basis. One of the ways to check in is through regular self-care practices that allow us to relax, to be in a state of flow and sense how we are doing.

## The Domestic Goddess Archetype

The Domestic Goddess archetype values her family. She has a labradoodle, two cats, and a wonderful husband. Down to the white picket fence, it's the perfect family. They are a goal-oriented couple that prioritizes growth and achievement.

They work a lot because they want to be very successful. They had more time for fun before they were married, but now they value being responsible, and task oriented most of the time.

The Domestic Goddess is organized and works hard to make sure everyone has what they need. She does all the cooking, cleaning, and organizing. She also works full time. She makes homemade food for her pets, using only organic ingredients.

She is constantly researching tips in organization and household management. Her house is beautifully styled and arranged. It was featured in a local decorating magazine. She does all the shopping for both her and her hubby. He doesn't have time for such things. He doesn't even buy his own underwear. She buys all his clothing, including underwear, and if it doesn't suit him, she takes care of the returns. Cooking is one of her fortes. She always uses the best ingredients, and she can convert any recipe to any size, accommodating to any allergy or taste preference. It's just one of her skills.

Sure, there's a lot on her plate, but it's worth the sacrifice. It's better than her childhood where she had parents who suffered from alcohol addictions. Knowing things could be much worse, she pushes through her days and always does her best.

She loves to paint, dance, and go to yoga, but she doesn't have time for that anymore. She was in a book club a couple of years ago but has since stopped going because she just doesn't have the time. She tends to put her projects and down-time on hold. Taking time for yourself is a luxury for those who have it all together. One day she will have it all, she tells herself. For now, though, time is valuable, and she needs to keep up with the important stuff.

Her in-laws don't really like her, but she tries to impress them. She still holds onto childhood trauma, so she is used to drama and feeling unsafe. She's always striving for acceptance, but it never comes, no matter how many hours she pours into making food they like or trying to be cordial when they are around. Maybe they withhold love because she is acting so desperate to win their acceptance.

After several years of all the busy-ness, she's unhealthy, unhappy, and disconnected from her purpose. She feels low, and disempowered. Her self-esteem decreases all the time. Maybe this is because she never makes time to take care of herself. She feels like nothing is really moving forward in her life. She wonders why. Her husband's career as a politician is skyrocketing each year. She wonders what's wrong with herself, why can't she seem to move forward at such a speed too.

She would like to connect more with her husband, but most of his downtime is spent socializing for his career. She is alone a lot. Sometimes she feels undervalued, but she's not sure what to do. She tries to rekindle their love, but often, things are lackluster. He's usually busy or super tired. It's just the way things are.

While folding laundry and watching a talk show, a woman with a garish look and bold speaking style is waving her arms around and yelling at the crowd that they need to do what they truly love in this life. She speaks about it being your life, your rules. She stands on her chair and yells, "what the hell are you doing in your life that reflects you!?" Whoa. Somehow this lands. Maybe it was the theatrics and maybe it was the message.

Later that night she lies awake; she cannot get that image out of her head. She starts to wonder, what in the hell do I want? Hmm, she's not entirely sure. It's been a while since she's been to the botanical gardens, so she starts with that. She remembered seeing an advertisement about the lilacs being in bloom. This is one of her favorite spring flowers, so she decides to go to the botanical gardens.

On the way there she feels a bit of dread. Taking a couple hours out of her day to visit the botanical gardens felt like an act of defiance. Once she arrives at the gardens, she feels much better. She is in awe over all the beautiful flowers. She smiles as she remembers how much she loves being outside amongst the flowers and trees. As she strolls through the gardens, she further reflects on the question, what does she want out of life. It looks like she won't be having any kids. She could always get more pets. That could keep her busy, but was that enough? She decides that this time for strolling and getting in tune with herself was time spent on something valuable to her. She sets a goal to do this every day for the next month. Yeah, just like that, she decided to take time for herself.

The Domestic Goddess lets the home tasks slide for a month. She focuses on herself. In doing so, she takes back her time and energy. Instead of worrying about all the little and big tasks at home, she makes time for major introspection. She wonders about her day-to-day life. Does it bring out her best? Is her relationship balanced in a way that she wanted? Does she feel loved in this relationship? Eventually, she sees that her day-to-day actions are not in alignment with what she truly wants. She starts to seriously consider if there is anything in her relationship that is working for her.

After a month of visiting the gardens, her husband is confused. Why is the house such a mess? Why isn't the laundry done? What will he wear tomorrow? What's going on with the bathroom sink? Where are his favourite snacks? She sees his reaction to her taking time for herself and she's not sure there is any hope. She mentions that perhaps they need couples counseling. Initially, he's totally against it. What if anyone in the town finds out he's having marital troubles? His reply seals the deal. She's out. It was scary, but she sets her boundaries. She feels she must break up to break free and offer herself growth in her life.

After a few days, her husband wants to talk. He is interested in working it out. Really? Yes. He is willing to do what it takes to bring balance to their lives. She's both shocked and delighted.

They find suitable couple's counseling, and both strive to do what it takes to overcome their patterns. They decide to hire a weekly cleaning service to help take some of the pressure off as they establish new habits in their relationship. They buy a robotic lawn mower for the yard. Their relationship blossoms with new energy and they both feel more like themselves in the relationship.

She starts attending a Co-Dependents Anonymous group in her town. She also continues to take her daily walks to the botanical gardens throughout the year. She loves each season, especially spring and summer to see the new flowers in bloom each week. Over time, she realizes that the rewards she receives from self-care are far greater than the time and energy self-care practices take. She goes from thinking it was all on her to focusing on herself. She transformed from The Domestic Goddess to The Self-Care Queen.

## Consider the possibility that when you choose yourself, the Universe takes notice and responds accordingly.

All work and no time to unwind can lead to nervous system and physical issues. A balanced life requires a regular tuning into intuition, and releasing of emotions and feelings, time for the nervous system to relax, exposure to new patterns, sights, and sounds. Unstructured time in inspiring spaces, such as nature, is especially helpful for creativity. And while you can relax and recalibrate and implement self-care practices that cultivate self-love in a variety of settings, nature connection with the more-than-human-world offers so much all at once.

Staying in tune with who you are is essential if you have a tendency to over-give or lose yourself in other people's projects. How can you do this? Practice feeling your feelings, explore your emotions, ground and center, relax, think creatively, and sense into your inner knowing. This inner knowing or intuition is key. Your intuition is always guiding you, steering you from relationships and experiences that may not be the best for you. Making time to tune into intuition may seem like it would take time away from producing something, it may seem like it would take time away from growth, but tuning in helps you stay focused on what really matters to you. It helps you live authentically, make better decisions, and contributes to you being able to make the most of your time at work and in your personal life.

Spending time in nature is necessary for good health and psychological well-being. Making the most of this time in nature by tuning in to your intuition makes sense. Many, if not all of us, need both. We need to spend time in nature, and we need to make time for self-care that is centring, grounded and helping us tune into our intuition. Nature provides a dynamic space that encourages creativity and problem solving. So, on many levels, it makes sense to combine tuning into yourself and spending time in nature.

Spending 120 minutes in nature each week for nature connection is as important as brushing your teeth each day.

In this book, the focus is not on changing or challenging your problems, your relationships. This is not about the person who might be dimming your light. It's not about the problems that arise. This practice works at the root, creating a strong foundation at the core. It focuses on you. It focuses on that which is in your power to change. You are the one you can change. You can commit to becoming more of who you are and who you are meant to be. You can then choose how you will respond to your world, all of it. The daily practice of nature connection creates a stronger, more positive sense of self, and supports bringing you back to feeling higher vibe emotions. It is a daily practice that creates the space for positive change in your life. It helps you shine.

# Chapter Five

## Self-Love

Some may confuse selfishness with self-love. Selfishness is living for yourself and yourself alone. A scarcity mindset and viewing people as either winners or losers is a big part of the motivation in selfishness.

## From Self-Centered to Self-Loving: The Influencer Wifey Archetype

It's like the archetype I will call Influencer Wifey. She's the best, no one compares to her, she's flawless. Even though you've got to fight to have it, and there's not enough to go around, she's got it. She doesn't have many real friends, she only values people if they can do something for her. If they can't, let's face it, they're useless.

She loves social media. She has a knack for creating the best posts and reels. She gets a phenomenal number of likes. Influencer Wifey posts many times a day because she needs outside validation to feel good. She believes she knows everything about self-care. She can tell you anything you need to know about spa treatments, hair and makeup styling, fillers, plastic surgeries, and having perfect nails. People can learn it all from this Instagram Influencer. Her IG account oozes in luxurious self-care, and it is full of exclusive lifestyle self-care tips. She has nearly one million followers. She's better than any of the other influencers she knows, and she loves being at the top. She's always fought hard to be the best.

She feels so empty without praise and constant recognition. It can be a very rough day if she doesn't get enough attention. She hates seeing anyone do well in the world and can be jealous or angry when her friends post about their success. If they are doing well, it means that she must push herself to do more.

In her personal life, she manipulates people into saying and doing nice things for her. She usually expects too much of others and she feels supremely rejected if people don't respond the way she wants. She's never been completely satisfied with life and always strives for more. It's not her fault the world is this way, it's everyone else's fault when anything goes wrong.

One day she arrives home to her loft to find a note. Her incredibly hot, chiseled, rich husband is leaving her. He is also very superficial and decides he doesn't want to be married anymore. In his note he states he's done. If she needs anything, forget about him, he'll be clubbing in Miami. Classic, she thinks, so classic. She pins the failure of her marriage 100% on her husband, though deep down she knows they didn't have that much in common, other than the fact that they were both so good looking.

To take her mind off the divorce, she goes glamping with some influencer girlfriends. They stay at an exclusive resort with well-appointed yurts. The yurts are more like hotel rooms, complete with little fireplaces and air conditioning, amazing views from large picture windows, a mini bar, a jacuzzi tub, steam shower, and 24/7 full service. She feels super thrilled to be in nature, without it being too naturey.

While she's out on a hike she accidentally falls off the trail and down a small grassy hill. The fall knocks her out. When she wakes up, she is staring at a bear standing over her. The first instinct is to grab her phone and take a video for her stories. The bear snorts and she decides that this may not be the best idea. She sits there, looking up at the bear as it stares at her. There is this moment. All of a sudden, she feels very differently about her whole life, her decisions, even her award-winning IG account. She looks into the eyes of the bear, and even though things could go sideways in an instant she's not afraid. She feels like their exchange is like a conversation. Much to her surprise, she senses love and acceptance. There is a similarity, a connection between the two of them. One of the resort staff blasts on their whistle and the bear runs away. She gets up, feeling a little wobbly. At that moment, she decides she wants to spend more time in the woods.

She starts visiting the local forest on weekends. As she does, she meets new people. It's a different crowd than she is used to. In her mind, they have zero fashion sense, but they are so nice and welcoming. It feels like a genuine connection. She has more encounters with forest animals, starts to notice all the different types of birds, and sees the beautiful trees and plants in a new way. Overall, she begins to feel more relaxed and accepting of herself. She's a little less concerned with outside appearances. She likes the feeling of calm she has after she visits greenspaces.

With time, she changes. She develops a stronger sense of love for herself. She views the world as more abundant. The connection she feels as she spends time in the forest expands the love, she has for all, including herself. From this new mindset, she is less competitive, and she is genuinely happy for others' success. She starts to care more for others. She needs less validation from others, and she changes the focus of her social media account to reflect content that is more authentic and less of a show. She starts to post things of value that will help others feel better about themselves. Initially, she lost quite a few followers, but she was okay with that. Eventually, things pick up again, but with an entirely new vibe and she connects many new positive and kind people with IG accounts in the process. She is so impressed by the depth and beauty she finds in her new positive connections. She is sincerely overjoyed by other's success she reads about. From a place of abundance, she can offer more empathy when others are struggling. And you know, she's simply happier each day. Her outlook has transformed a great deal!

She becomes more honest with herself. She is willing to admit her flaws and begins to see that her quirks make her unique. She starts to do mirror work where she affirms to herself some of her positive traits while looking in the mirror. She can give more compliments to others. She works on herself and takes responsibility for her own well-being and happiness. She is so proud of how far she's come. She celebrates each accomplishment.

An old friend texts her to tell her that her ex is dating someone way younger, extremely good looking, and very famous due to her all-new lasers, and deep-sea rare plant extract spa line. Apparently, she's endorsed by a few celebs. It stuns Influencer Wifey that the old friend only texts to share these stories, but it doesn't bother her like it would have in the past.

That night, she takes some time under the full moon and sets the intention to forgive herself. She knows that her former self was doing the best at the time. She didn't know what she knows now. And now she's doing better. She forgives her ex. It's easy because her life is better. She forgives the old friend with the news. All in all, that night, she lets go of her old life. She is finally able to let go of the hurt from the divorce, and she moves on to live in the present.

She has the best sleep and wakes up the next morning knowing her past has many lessons. She's grateful to move on feeling better about herself. She lets go of hurt from the past and she remains hopeful for her future. She has a better idea of what she's looking for in her intimate relationships. He's got to love spending time in nature. Until she meets someone she can truly connect with, she's totally okay on her own.

One day, after a few years of regular visits to the forest, she's completely new. Old friends don't even recognize her. She hasn't made as much time for the intense upkeep with spa treatments as she once did, and she's older, but she feels better, and she looks better than before. Who knew that a glow from the inside, reflecting true happiness, kindness towards the world, is beautiful too. She transforms from Influencer Wifey to the Lass of True, Ever-Expanding Self-Love.

# Chapter Six

## Self-Love Sparks from Within and Lights Up Your World

The self-love we cultivate in nature connection is rooted in an expanding abundance mindset. This is because connection with nature reminds you of the goodness in you and beyond yourself. The view changes. Quite literally, instead of the world revolving around your selfish self, you are immersed in it all and are a part of it all. Carl G. Jung illustrates this when he says, "At times I feel as if I am spread over the landscape and inside things, and am myself living in every tree, in the s plashing of the waves, in the clouds and the animals that come and go, in the procession of the seasons."

Building upon this, Ecologist Stephan Harding, PhD.,

explains "When we are thus "spread over the landscape," we feel nature is animate - that is imbued with intelligence, wisdom, and a communicative ability that makes us feel a natural inclination to minimize harm to the greater self that enfolds and nurtures us. From this level of consciousness, we make choices that minimize harm to the greater body of the Earth, which we experience as our own body. We opt for simplicity and frugality in our material consumption and cultivate richness and diversity in our cultural and spiritual lives, where we realize that true satisfaction lies."

A connection to nature makes us want to do better for the planet, and a connection to nature means we are a part of all we want to help. It naturally includes us too. For those of us with a history of over giving, I propose a slightly different angle than Harding presents. Nature connection helps us cultivate love for ourselves first. It helps us see ourselves in the beauty of it all and from here we can access so much goodness like peace, self-esteem, and curiosity. When we possess a vibrant and positive sense of self, we naturally do better in our relationships, do better for our communities, and for the planet. We work from a mindset of abundance that doesn't require depletion of the self to solve problems and show we care. There is a profound sense of care for all, including ourselves.

Starting with the self is not the same as self-centered when it is in the context of connection to all. It means we are healthy and at our best for ourselves first. We are the ones who can choose to change for the better. It is the area where we have the most influence. From an ever-expanding self-love we radiate out from our greater selves to be our best in our communities and ecosystems. It starts with you, in nature, but it's not selfish because you are paying attention to context and fostering healthy connections to life around you.

Self-Love in this guide is about a to-the-core self-recognition, self-acceptance and self-understanding that supports authenticity as you relate to your world. It is about seeing yourself as continually connected to that which is larger than you. It is about realizing personal purpose within a larger context. Self-love reminds us why we are here, and that the self is a part of larger ecosystems and contributes to larger ecosystems. In this, you are more compassionate and loving towards yourself. What does it look like to be the best, most actualized, authentic versions of yourself? Regular interactions with nature can help you understand, accept and love yourself in a deeper way.

And from here, you get to choose your feeling state destination. What is the message your presence and actions radiate out into the world? You can choose. An abundance of joy, resilience, happiness, and connection are all possible in your vision of self-love. What do you need to sustain yourself through the storms of life? This vision of self-love goes beyond the list of self-care rituals you can add to your life. It's not a glass of pinot noir and a bubble bath. Oh noooo, you deserve more than that. It is a vision for your life. Nature connection can help you remain focused on what really matters in your life and what you need to sustain yourself within this larger ecosystem of your life and even the planet.

## Some of what your vision may include:

Joy
Freedom
Happiness
Love
Prosperity
Connection
Light

What is your vision of self-love? Write it down, add emotions that exude positivity, and put it where you can read it every day.

# Chapter Seven

## Setting Intentions

## Creating Personal Transformation If You Tend to Over-give.

Consider the fact that no one will ever completely understand what it takes to be you.

No one knows what it takes to care for you. It may be possible that people will not understand your need to take time out. They might not understand what it takes to overcome and work through your trauma, to do your personal work. They won't see it unless you mention it and even then, they might not understand. You can't expect support from people who benefit from seeing you playing small or dimming your light. They might interpret your self-care as laziness or resistance when you are fighting with everything you've got to improve.

You are the captain of your ship. And you are in it until the end. You are the one there for you through thick and thin. People might think they know what's best for you, but you get to decide what's best for you. You are the owner of it all, your failings and victories.

It's the hardest to maintain your hope when everything seems to be going in the wrong direction. You become an easy target. I mean, look at the proof, right? You will see it too, and that can make the advice and opinions of others more compelling. People might comment that your life is going downhill and that you are focusing on the wrong things. You don't have to listen to anything, especially if it seeds doubt. Ask yourself: are they adding to doubt and subtly eroding your self-esteem or are they helping you reach your goals?

People trying to transform need space and support, not panicked advice or judgments that add to fear, overwhelm and can halt you in your tracks. Even Oprah, a verified success, has people in her life with all the advice. The difference is that she already has proof she can make it. She's made it. When you haven't made it, you need to be strong, maybe stronger than Oprah and believe in yourself.

Creating transformation in your life requires a strong commitment to yourself. You will make it if you give it your all. When things seem to be going the wrong direction, you've got to double down on your own alignment. What does that mean? Get crystal clear on what you want, affirm it many times a day, and believe you can do it. Don't stop until you arrive. Use any tool you can to get there.

A good example to illustrate this is weight loss. In my experience, food and weight are complicated in that it's not only about the food. It's way more than calories in calories out. My best weight loss programs have been break-ups, ha-ha. All jokes aside, my success in weight loss was due to stress reduction. I was successful in the end when I was able to stress less and focus on myself. By allowing this first, I was more open to eating the foods I needed, and participating in the activities that made my body feel great. Yes, my body responds well to exercise, but as we all know, exercise alone doesn't do it. All the efforting, shame, guilt, promises, plans, programs, self-loathing, and judgy comments from others did nothing. I needed to relax and let this animal (me) feel safe. I needed to tune into me and then I could transform.

## This guide is written with the principles of personal transformation in mind. What are some of the necessary steps to take to successfully adopt new habits that lead to more of what we want?

1.    Decide what you want and where you want to go. You are the person to determine this. What is your goal? Have a vision in mind and write it down. Read this vision, out loud when you can, each day. Imagine how you will feel when you achieve your goal. Use a tracker to chart your progress. You are more likely to see your success if you track your actions each day.

2.    Take steps each day to reach your goal. Be aware of your energy levels and keep it fun. It is easier to achieve a goal with small, consistent daily actions than pushing through with sporadic and heroically huge moves. Don't try to do it all in one day. When you are in the habit of tuning into your energy each day, you will find there are days when your energy is high, and you can do more and then there are days when your energy is lower, and you might not be able to do as much. Embrace the moment. Keep going but go easy on yourself when your energy

is low.  Enjoy doing more when you have higher energy levels. Don't be derailed if you miss a day, stay positive, even if you need to start again with smaller daily actions.

3.    Seek out stories of people who have accomplished what you are setting out to do.  Get curious and look for stories of transformation. Find proof that others have done what you are doing. Research what this meant to them.  Learn from their mistakes.

4.    Be, Do, Have.  Be the person you want to be.  Make the change today.  Imagine how you will feel, and how you will carry yourself when you have achieved the goal and start imagining like it has already happened.

5.    Be willing to be a little uncomfortable. Embodying a new way of being involves change and it can feel scary to face change.  You don't have to go into the eye of the storm to create major change. You can, but it is not necessary.  Change occurs at the edge of comfortability as well.  Each day do things that you intuitively know will bring you closer to the change you want to see.  Count to ten and make your move. Do it daily.

6.    Be your own support system.  Don't be blinded by the light of others and their advice.  And don't rely on others to light your way.  You are a star, you've got this.  It's great when people understand you and your goals but let's face it, they might not always get what you do.  They may even be against what you want to do because they can resist change, even good change, in you too.  The most important person who needs to understand and support you is you.

It's important to develop a strong belief in yourself, your intuition, and your personal journey.  Nature connection can help you to develop a strong belief in yourself, to believe in your power to light your way.

# Chapter Eight

## Step One of the Stellar Method

### SHED - old energies; feel your feelings, forgive, and move on.

### Name your feelings:

Do you feel sadness, fear, anger, disgust, joy or something else?

What can you do today to bring you more joy and peace?

Get to know yourself through the practice of feeling your feelings.

By taking the time to regularly feel your feelings, and naming your feelings, you are getting to know yourself better. You will then be better able to articulate your feelings for yourself and you will see more clearly how you feel in your relationships. Adopting the healthy practice of feeling and naming your feelings, and practicing regulating your emotions is key in overcoming codependency.

As you let go of codependency, you will discover more about yourself: your likes, dislikes, wants and needs. Being authentically you will offer more contentment and a happier state of being.

Step one is all about starting where you are. It is about taking time to feel your feelings, and honestly naming them. You do this with compassion and care.

When I am in the city, I will usually walk to a park or forest to nature connect. As I walk to my destination, and as I move my body, I find that my feelings come up and out. I'm more aware of what I'm feeling as I walk to the greenspace. It can be surprising because I may not notice any lingering sadness or anger in my body until I get outside.

Whether you walk to the greenspace or not, start by asking yourself how you are feeling. As my friend Éva says, "the forest is a safe space where we can feel." Greenspaces are living spaces that offer an opportunity to sense more within us.

## Step One is SHED. It is about addressing what you are feeling now and letting go of what you do not need.

Feelings are good. Feelings are a bodily reaction to your internal or external environments. Feelings carry a message that reveals what you need. Our natural, healthy high-vibing state is happiness. The message your feelings convey will help you understand what you need to find your way back to joy. Modern studies have shown that a feeling is physical. They carry an electromagnetic charge. With the right tools we can see it. Feelings are frequencies, and there are lower vibing feelings and higher vibing feelings. Can you guess which ones are high-vibing, sparkling states, and which ones are low-vibing, tangled, or stagnant states?

The goal in feeling your feelings is to identify what you are feeling. Then, if you want to or if you need to, you can ask yourself what it will take to bring yourself back to a higher emotional state. This is a skill that can be practiced and mastered.

It's important to find yourself in the higher vibing states as much as possible. The way you feel influences the health of the body, the ways you respond to life, and your self-perception. The way you feel influences the way you experience and re-spond to life. It's huge.

There are five major feeling constellations; sadness, fear, anger, disgust, and joy.

It is helpful to respect your feelings, to move or sit with them, and try not to react or judge. Observe yourself and simply feel into the feelings. Breathe. Do this in a loving, gentle and kind way. You can hug yourself or hug a tree as you feel your feelings, and remind yourself that you are connected. When you allow your feelings to mature in a supportive, loving way, you can find your way back to joy and relief.

• If you feel sadness, it could be that your body is telling you that there is a loss of love or you need more love.

• If you feel fear, it could be that your body is telling you that you are not safe and you need to find safety.

• If you feel anger, it could be that your body is telling you that your boundaries were violated and you need to set better boundaries.

- If you feel disgust, it could be that your body is telling you that someone or something is wrong for you.

- If you feel joy, it could be that your body is telling you that you want more of the same.

Identify the feeling and ask what you need to do to bring things back to joy, then do one thing that will move you in the direction back to joy and relief. Even the smallest shift can help. It is important to be able to do it for yourself. It should offer you a sense of relief and it should feel like it is from a place of love.

Remember, this is a daily practice. You don't have to do everything in one day. The goal is to be in the practice of feeling your feelings and to make small shifts each day. Make it easy, relax, a huge difference can be made over time.

## Understanding the difference between a belief vs. a feeling vs. an emotion is essential.

A belief is a thought form. It is an opinion, it is not based on facts, and it can often be wrong. Any belief about yourself that leaves you feeling disconnected are probably not true.

## If a belief is true, it is a TRUTH.

## The six primary beliefs, spanning positive and negative, and the positives are TRUTH:

I am worthy, or I am unworthy.
I am good, or I am evil.
I am loveable, or I am not loveable.
I am deserving, or I am undeserving.
I am powerful, or I am powerless.

I have value, or I have no value.
I am connected, or I am separate.

## BELIEF + FEELING = EMOTION ==> over a sustained time creates a PARADIGM

A belief + a feeling = an emotion. They are described as energy in motion. We allow the feeling to tell a story, and these stories may not be facts. When a belief and a feeling are held together for long enough, they create a paradigm. What I mean by paradigm is the mostly unseen lens by which we end up viewing the world. These unseen lenses can be limiting or empowering. It can be difficult to dismantle a paradigm. Cyndi Dale describes these thoughts as strings of pearls that form pathways in our neurological system. These networks of opinions or beliefs form patterns that can make us feel stuck.

Feeling our feelings and being able to label them helps to dismantle or wriggle loose one part of the equation in creating a paradigm. The simple practice of feeling your feelings can help dismantle sticky paradigms and limiting beliefs that can hold you back and cause you to feel stuck. The more you allow your feelings to mature by naming them and feeling them, and bring yourself back to a space where you can ask yourself what you really want, the better you will be at releasing your patterns and beliefs that leave you stuck.

To heal a feeling, name it and feel it. Ask yourself what you need right now to take a small step back to joy, relief, happiness, gratitude, calm, bliss, delight, wonder, charm, harmony, tranquility, and serenity.

As I've mentioned, it is usually not a once and done type task. You benefit from daily doses of actions and affirmations that bring us back to joy. Nature connection is a perfect way to bring us back to joy on a regular basis.

On my walks, in the company of the more-than-human-world, these feelings tend to transmute, sometimes without much effort. But I do tend to need to get outside, away from my daily tasks, on my journey back to the forest before I can feel, understand what I need, and work towards feeling better. This practice helps me understand what I need from day to day.

Peace and joy are the places where you want to be most of the time.

## WHAT CAN YOU DO TODAY TO BRING YOU MORE JOY AND PEACE?

One of the best ways to allow more joy and peace is to let it go. When you visit a greenspace regularly and offer forgiveness, you can choose to leave a little bit of your grief and trauma behind. Let it be compost for the earth. It doesn't have to be everything in one day, but bit by bit, if you leave a little, soon you will have left a lot.

### Emotional Guidance Scale

I'm sending you good vibes. What do I mean by that? It's my shorthand for actual higher vibrational states that are not associated with any religion.

Psychiatrist and researcher Dr. David R. Hawkins popularized the idea that emotions can be placed on a scale, demonstrating that higher vibrational states are associated with positive emotions such as joy, peace and happiness and negative emotions vibrate at a lower frequency. Positive emotions are believed to have higher vibrational frequencies than lower, or negative emotions. This idea is also found in ancient wisdom and threads of it are in several fields of modern science including psychology, neuroscience, and quantum physics. It seems obvious in a way, right? When you are in higher vibrational states, you're having a better time in whatever we are doing, right? It's not difficult to see that spending more time in these higher vibrational or positive emotional states are associated with greater success in life, and health.

In practical terms, you can change your vibrational state by eating whole, fresh food, breathing, expressing gratitude and being generous, meditating, singing, dancing, Reiki and other energy medicine therapies, moving the body in yoga or classical stretching, healthy relationships, and spending time in nature! Anything in your life that brings you back to peace and happiness is contributing to higher vibrational states.

I have studied with energy medicine experts such as Denise Linn and Cyndi Dale, and I use their teachings to empower me and help me remember I am the creator of my reality. If I boil it down, these teachings to one golden nugget of wisdom that I have needed my whole life: intention is everything.

## You are powerful. Your intentions are HUGE in creating your life.

You can choose your vibrational state through your intentions. Your imagination can alter the past, the future, and the present. You can affirm that light and love to flow in your life. Your vision for your life and your imagination  impacts your life. In fact, your imagination playd a powerful role in your life.

Vision-boards work. Posting affirmations to your bathroom mirror work. In 2007, for example, I manifested a gray fluffy cat, without even trying, when I posted a photo to my bathroom mirror of an adorable gray fluffy kitten who looked like he was in a spotlight on a stage. To me, he symbolized optimism. I absolutely loved this photo and I would look at it while brushing my teeth.  A few months later, a homeless gray fluffy cat arrived at my condo. Amazing, right?

Your thoughts, imagination and affirmations can bring to life the things you want whether that is health, prosperity, happiness, or a cat! On the flipside, worry and anxiety can manifest the opposite. In part, this is because affirmations will train the reticular activating system of the brain to see what you affirm. What you are experiencing, in part, was manifested by you. If you want greater success in all areas, create the intention to bring yourself back to a higher vibrational state. You will face challenges in this life, but if you intend to be in a higher vibing state you will naturally handle it better.

It's all about keeping it real. Sense into your emotions and your feelings. Explore and name them. Be authentic. When you find yourself in a lower vibe, be compassionate and do what you can.

Pay attention to the birds tweeting around you, notice the light glimmering from the dew on the leaves, or feel into the exact moment of the season. Noticing something small can help get you back on the road to peace and happiness. Spending time in dynamic greenspaces each day supports a high vibe state day after day.

Do you need help imagining where you would like to be in terms of your vibrational state? The emotional guidance scale below is used to help identify patterns and tendencies in an emotional terrain. Locate where you are at a particular moment, or generally. Then, with compassion, ask how you might be able to move to a higher emotional state most of the time or in a particular moment. It is a dance; you can skip multiple rungs in either direction. You can decide where you want to be most of the time, but life tends to be better, and you get more of what you want out of life, when you reside most of the time in higher emotional states.

## The Abraham-Hicks Emotional Guidance Scale

· Joy/Appreciation/Empowerment/Freedom/Love
· Passion
· Enthusiasm/Eagerness/Happiness
· Positive Expectation/Belief
· Optimism
· Hopefulness
· Contentment
· Boredom
· Pessimism
· Frustration/Irritation/Impatience
· Overwhelm
· Disappointment
· Doubt
· Worry
· Blame
· Discouragement
· Anger
· Revenge
· Hatred/Rage
· Jealousy
· Insecurity/Guilt/Unworthiness
· Fear/Grief/Desperation/Despair/
  Powerlessness

# Chapter Nine

## Step Two

## TRUST - in your connection to the Universe.

The ability to see tangible examples of goodness in your life helps you to trust your connection to the Universe. It helps to be grateful and to practice feeling grounded and connected.

## GRATITUDE & GROUNDING INTO THE ELEMENTS

Many years ago, I was sitting in a friend's backyard after dark and admiring a giant spruce tree. I was looking at it, thinking about my life, practicing gratitude for all the goodness in my life. Suddenly, a guy who sounds just like my brother is walking by with his friends. I call his name, and he replies. Much to my surprise it was my brother walking through the woods, at night, right behind this house! It was an incredible moment because I had not seen my brother for a few months. I didn't plan on being in that city that weekend. It was a last-minute decision to be there. I had no idea my brother was in that part of town. I wasn't asking for this, but I was sending him good energy. It was such a gift of connection at a time when I needed it.

## Trust and Gratitude

Step Two is to TRUST the universe, the divine, or God. Trust that the universal truths include you too: you are loved, you are worthy, you are good, you are deserving, you are powerful, you have value, and you are connected. One way to anchor the TRUTH is to recognize the tangible examples of goodness in your life. GRATITUDE is a practice that allows you to see what's working in our life. It offers psychological, physical and social benefits. It helps you see more clearly the support network around you. With regular gratitude, rumination decreases and is replaced with optimistic thoughts. It helps you see the things in your life that are working in your best interest.

When you practice seeing the good in your life, you increase your happiness, and life satisfaction. Gratitude improves your relationships, increasing love, care, hope, and your ability to forgive others. It improves our ability to learn, make decisions, and focus on solutions. Gratitude decreases anxiety and depression.

A daily gratitude practice offers a grounded focus, accepting the present, even during harsh times. In a word, it is awesome.

Exercise: Think of 5 things you are grateful for and say it out loud when you are nature connecting.

## Using Your Imagination to Ground into The Elements

| Element | Ground into an imaginal element. How do you feel when you ground into the element? Sense into it. The list below reflects some common associations people make with each element. Your feeling or experience may reflect something else, and that's okay. |
|---|---|
| Water | Purifies, cleanses, fluid and mobile, soothes and heals, feminine, enhances intuition, emotions, adaptability, depth, renewal, healing, growth, wisdom. |
| Fire | Strengthens, eliminates, protects, purges, purifies, burns away, transforms, adds vitality, masculine, encourages movement, passion, joy, builds, heals. |
| Earth | Builds, protects, soothes, cools, repairs, midnight, winter, new moon, feminine, representing potential and transformation, ready for creation, stable foundation for life. |
| Air | When active, it transmits ideas and energy from place to place or person to person, fast, blinking in and out of existence, intelligence, new beginnings, youth, creativity, spring, waxing moon, sunrise, active. |
| Metal | Protects, defends and deflects energy, geometrically shaped, conduit, precious. |

| Wood | Friendly, joyous, humorous, abundant, adaptable, warm, helpful. |
|------|------|
| Stone | Strengthens, protects, gemstones reflect the energy of the colour of the gemstone, will help to remove issues or emotions if you ask the stone to do so. |
| Ether | The in-between, wisdom, spirit, spirals, circles, foggy, can be used to infuse, Fifth element, holds spiritual truths. |
| Light | Electromagnetic radiation of various wavelengths that can produce a visual sensation, luminous, emitting or reflecting light, sun and sunlight, the speed of light. "Dark" light is associated with intelligence about power, "light" light is intelligence about love. Light can be called upon and directed. Scalar waves, absolute light, virtual light. |
| Sound | Vibration that travels through gas, liquid and objects, commences vibrational change, mechanical wave that represents power, a sensation, sound healing, sound baths, sounds in nature, bees buzzing, echolocation used by bats, whales, dolphins. |
| Star | Spiritual truth, truth, we are made of stardust. |
| Presence | Oneness, God, Universe, Tree of Life, Holy Spirit. |

After gratitude, you can practice grounding yourself into the elements. Often a grounding exercise is about grounding into the earth. To do this you imagine roots coming out of your feet or body and growing down into the earth. You breathe in and out and feel yourself centered and rooted.

Did you know that you can ground into many different elements to help in different ways? Try grounding into an element that suits your needs. Choose an element that will help you. There are no rules, other than to be smart about it. If you are suffering from too much heat, for example, a sunburn, don't ground into imaginal fire. If it's winter and you are freezing, you might want to ground into a little fire.

# Chapter Ten

## Step Three

**EXPLORE - remain curious, and get to know the multi-faceted diamond you are. Practice nature consciousness and get to know yourself within the ecosystem by:**

- tuning into your senses.

- experiencing surprises, inspiring awe.

- creating heart connections with trees and plants.

Cedar from 2020
I WANT TO SPEAK THE LANGUAGE OF CEDAR
ANCIENT AND AWARE
I WANT TO SPEAK THE LANGUAGE OF CEDAR
PROTECTOR AND FRIEND
I WANT TO SPEAK THE LANGUAGE OF CEDAR
READY TO SERVE AS A PERCH FOR BIRDS, AN
AMUSEMENT PARK FOR SQUIRRELS,
AN ELEVATOR FOR CATS,
AND TEA FOR HUMANS.
I WANT TO SPEAK THE LANGUAGE OF CEDAR
ROOTED AND AROMATIC
STEADY AND CONFIDENT.
AT THE FRONT DOOR
USHERING US THROUGH.
I WANT TO SPEAK THE LANGUAGE OF CEDAR.
BEAUTIFUL LIMBS
FINDING A WAY TO MY HEART
UNTANGLING MY ANXIOUS THREADS.

The Stellar method of nature connection is a way of practicing mindfulness. Mindfulness is a moment-by-moment awareness of your thoughts, feelings, bodily sensations, and surrounding environment through a gentle, nurturing lens. By focusing on the present you free yourself from worry and rumination. You let yourself be in flow in the here and now. In doing so, you bring down anxiety and allow for more positive emotions.

You will be more relaxed after the first two steps that include naming your feelings, offering gratitude and grounding. Being more relaxed will allow you to be more receptive in this next step to explore a peaceful nature connection. The Explore step is to tune into your senses so you can tune into nature.

## Tuning Into Your Senses Nature Connection Prompt

Take 1 - 20 minutes to sense what you are sensing. If you are short on time, set your timer, and put your phone down.

Slow down, either walk slowly, lean against a tree, or rest in complete stillness, and ask yourself what you can sense. What can you see, hear, taste, touch, and smell? How are you feeling in your body? What does it feel like to be your body in this space? Focus on each of the senses and see if you pick up on different aspects of the environment. Notice the air, the temperature, the noise, the light, and life around you. This step may bring up new aspects of your emotions and feelings. You may notice you are tired, or you are wired. You may see that the weather influences your mood. Try to find words that describe the moment. Simply recognizing what is, even beyond words, can be super helpful too. When you slow down and take the time to sense, you may sense other things such as your intuition. Tune in and trust yourself.

Exploring what you sense helps you to experience the moment in a full way and to understand yourself within the context of where you are and who surrounds you. As you tune into your surroundings, you may enter a liminal space, perhaps you can compare it to a meditative space.

Nurture your own unconditional self-love. Visiting a greenspace is a small act of self-love. Nature reminds you that everything is beautiful and acceptable, just as it is, including you. A tree doesn't need validation to feel like a tree. A tree is a tree, and you are you. A tree isn't less of a tree if it is not perfect. The same goes for you. You can breathe and be. You are lovable, valuable, and beautiful, even if you are not perfect.

## Creating your own original nature connection invitations

In forest therapy, invitations are another way to explore the moment. There is no wrong way of responding to an invitation. An invitation opens you to the moment and allows you to sense.

The best invitations are simple, open and sensory. The essence of an invitation includes an action verb, a sensory verb, and the more-than-human-world.

### Examples of action verb + sensory verb + and more-than-human-world invitations:

Stroll out + and notice + the little things in the forest around you.

Look up + and watch + the clouds above.

Stretch out your arm + and feel + the snowflakes falling.

Winter is a time of quiet rest and renewal.
I invite you to wander out and,
with an open heart,
feel the stillness
of this season.

## MOMENTS OF AWE are like glimmers.

Glimmers are moments during your day that evoke joy. When in nature, a moment of awe may occur when you find something beautiful or surprising. You may find it in patterns or anomalies. It might be a sound in the greenspace, such as the call of a bird. It could be a surprise encounter with a creature great or very small. Tune into all your senses, look for what is big and small, look for textures, sense in the light around you. Look up and look down. What is in motion around you, slow moving or lightning quick? Describe the air around you; is it windy or still? When you are tuned into your senses you are more likely to sense awe.

## HEART CONNECTIONS WITH THE MORE THAN HUMAN WORLD.

Nature connection is relational. We often talk about the benefits we receive in nature connection, but it is a relational activity that offers more than the benefits available to humans.

One way to be in relation with nature is to practice heart connections with trees. I originally heard about this from Denise Linn. The following describes how I do it. Allow your body to slow down and allow your senses to tune into the space around you. Find a tree that you are drawn to. Say hello to the tree, do you sense an openness in return? If so, keep going. It can be a big tree or a small tree. It should have a good feeling to it, something about it that is appealing to you. Focus on this tree in view. Imagine sending love from your heart to the plant or tree. Breathe and focus on the tree. Allow yourself to relax and sense into the moment. Imagine love in a bubble or in waves and imagine it floating towards the tree. Then wait. What happens after that is pretty cool. You may receive a sense of love in return. Surprisingly, there can be a touch of humor, laughter, or joy to it as well.

For the first time you try this, I suggest you try this when you are feeling good. Find a tree that has a nice feeling or energy to it. You can use this technique with all sorts of plants. So, talk to your plants. Since 1900, and likely even earlier than this, experiments have been conducted that prove plants like feeling our positive intentions. Plants respond well to our love.

What's interesting here is that you can develop a relationship with the trees you offer heart connections. Trees can be like friends, a supportive presence in our lives. Sometimes you can relate to a tree as you would a friend. You can share more than love. You can also leave your burdens. If you are feeling sad, start by greeting the tree. Ask if you can share with the tree. Wait for a response, and then share what's going on. You might want to ask for assistance in laying your burdens, composting your cares, or transmuting them. Transmuting in this case, means to allow them to dissolve or imagining them dissipating to other realms. Even if these are symbolic gestures for you, they can offer relief. Remember, there is power in your intentions. Trees can offer friendship. And you can offer your friendship to trees too. You can tune into messages from trees. Be a good friend to trees. Don't only leave burdens, leave love, spend time with the trees. And if you see a tree suffering, you can offer help too.

Your roots go deep.
You are protected.
You can weather anything.
- Denise Linn

# Chapter Eleven

## Step Four

### LISTEN - to your intuition.

A couple years ago I was practicing being okay in my skin, loving myself, taking care of myself with daily exercise. I felt complete, but every day I faced what felt like a deficiency of affection in my relationships. I didn't know this at the time, but I was relying on others for validation. Some of the important relationships I was in were not able to provide this. And then one day I was surprised by an incredible experience with crows following me as I walked down from the Summit Woods in Montreal. It felt nice to see them circling above me again and again as I made my way around each corner. I wondered if there was a message in this. All I really sensed in the company of the crows was connection and acceptance. A few minutes later I was in a store, and I had an unusual conversation with the cashier. He was talking about what he valued in life. Then he said, "You are beautiful just as you are. You don't need anyone to complete you." When he said that, it felt like the message from the crows. The experience with the crows and the message from this man matched in terms of timing and feeling. My message for the day was that I was worthy of love, and I am loved and accepted by Source. I was offered hope that life will sort itself out. Though messages from nature might not be this obvious or exact, they often reflect positive themes that help you move along in life, and that help you grow.

Step Four is to LISTEN to your intuition. Intuition is the knowledge available to you that is beyond conscious reasoning. This instinctive sense is available to us because our bodies are "complex and sensitive intuitive receptor(s)" within a biofield that extends beyond the physical boundaries of the body. With practice, most of us can access useful information available through our intuition.

## Your intuition can speak through:

## Clairaudience offering audible messages.

## Clairvoyance presenting something you see.

## Clairsentience as a feeling.

## Claircognizance presenting a knowing.

How do you know it is your intuition and not your mind chattering away? You know it's coming from your intuition when it lacks a charge such as anger, fear, anxiety, etc. Even if there is trouble and you need to move, there will be a steady energy to it and you will be compelled to move.

The previous steps of identifying your feelings, tuning into your heart, and exploring the space you are in, you are relaxed, grounded, hopefully feeling more positive, and open to receive clear messages. If you are in a negative or frazzled state, it can block your intuition.

Be open and try not to control it. Don't discredit unusual, or simple messages. It's your intuition if it helps you improve your life and encourages you to do good. You have power to decide how you will respond. It can be a good idea to follow it because you may not consciously understand what your unconscious mind can sense.

## SIGNS IN NATURE can help you receive messages from a greater knowing.

What would you consider to be a sign in nature? If you see something unusual and you have a feeling of calm or awe, it may be considered a sign. A sign for what? A clue that offers a little insight into life. Keep it clear, simple and honest.

Sometimes signs in nature are associated with bad omens. An animal sighting for example, might be associated with bad luck. It doesn't have to be this way. The sign should be safe for you and the animal. Anything that encourages fear and discrimination against animals should be questioned. No animal is a bad sign for anything. No colour is evil. It's okay to be curious about folk knowledge, but we must remember that we create and are responsible for our worldviews.

It's a better plan to focus on the Light. Let light guide you. Any sign will reflect a path towards growth and goodness. This isn't to say that there isn't a lesser vibe, low vibes, downright dirty vibes and intentions. The Light is greater than the darkness and it will always be enough to guide you.

Messages in nature, the ones that are of value to you, will be from Source. Source offers Light, Love, and Connection. It is information for you to be your best. It is not charged with worry, fear, and sadness. Anything it offers will help you make things better for yourself and for your world.

Some of the signs I have received in nature have included robins, toads, rainbows, snakes, bats, turkey vultures, crows, deer, wild turkeys, other birds, butterflies, fireflies, dragonflies and shooting stars. Generally, for me, it is something unusual, there will be a feeling in the air, and I will just know. When I saw a flock of over 10 robins, it felt very special. It causes me to stop and consider my life, my community, my flock.

When you spot a sign, the most important piece of information in deciphering what it means is how you feel when it happens.

Sure, there are countless websites offering info on what something might mean, but can you sense a message in the moment? Can you trust your own inner knowing? Remember, this is high vibe messaging. It should reflect love, light, or a solution to a problem in your life. There will be a steady feeling to it, reflecting truth.

## It ain't all sunshine and roses

## Part One: What we witness out there.

Some of the things we see in nature are painful to witness. These include seeing animals do things that we wouldn't do, destruction by weather events, and witnessing harm done by humans.

One day, I was full of sunshine and positivity, and I came across crows disturbing nests in trees, probably eating what was in the nests. It was difficult to watch but there are tough lessons in nature, too. These animals are behaving in their normal ways, and it can be upsetting to see how they behave. In these cases, I remain an observer and work through the truth in the way things are. It is a good idea to maintain a respect for the way beings choose to survive, to offer kindness and understanding, even if it challenges us.

At other times I have witnessed the destruction of trees in storms, such as ice storms. It is distressing to walk through after the damage is done, but it does make me reflect on life, how some live long, through many storms and some are here only for a short while. It reminds me of how our time here is finite and that it is a good idea to make the most of it. It also gives me a more profound respect for elders and all that they have weathered in life.

Very sadly, I have come across squirrels, and birds run over by cars. In these moments I offer respect and try to help in a safe way. Safety first, but I take the time to offer respect and to do what I can. In these cases, the message is not so much about our lives, but how we respond to the world around us. When beings suffer because of human actions, it is helpful to think of ways to solve these problems.

## It ain't all sunshine and roses

## Part Two: What we witness in ourselves.

Be aware of your inner dialogue. Name it if you find yourself engaged in negative self-talk, negative thinking, doubting yourself, and devaluing yourself. Breathe and let it go. Offer compassion towards yourself. Inch towards offering yourself kindness and understanding. If you find yourself spinning stories about the future, and falling into anxiety, like trying to predict the future and coming up with the worst-case scenarios, gently bring yourself back to focusing on your needs, feelings, desires, and values.

Are you noticing feelings of loneliness and abandonment? Nature has a way of reminding us that we are connected to something larger than ourselves. In a way, this helps diminish our fear of the future, fear of rejection, isolation and abandonment. Listen to your body. You may need time in nature and to reach out to a friend or professional. Don't hold back, you can have it all.

Do you feel stuck? The textures and abundant life found in greenspaces inspires creativity and flexibility. You may be inspired to dream a little bigger and inspired to new heights in personal growth. When you are in a relaxed state in nature, you are in the ideal state of mind to evaluate how you feel in all aspects of life, from personal life to professional goals. Allow nature to inspire, and again, if you need more, have the courage to seek out support.

## IS IT OKAY TO USE YOUR PHONE WHILE TUNING INTO NATURE?

### The Smartphone: how you might use this tool in nature connection

Not that long ago, I was quite critical of being attached to the cell phone during nature connection. Nature connection helps us unplug and tune into the world around us. It can be a break from the constant distraction of the phone.

Now, I must admit that I am a phone carrying nature

connector. I have shifted my perspective.

Like a lot of things, it is not the phone that is the problem. It's the human using the phone who needs to learn to manage their relationship with technology. It's a balance. You don't want to be using your phone the whole time and you don't want to not use it because it is a great tool to aid in nature connection. It has a timer and silence function, thereby offering you a break, if you let it do so. It's also a layer of security in being able to contact people quickly and efficiently if you run into any trouble.

## Ways to use your phone while nature connecting.

1) Silence notifications and set a timer. During busy weeks, with schedules and deadlines, it can help to know that you have a container holding your nature connection experience. Five minutes is great if that's all the time you have. Studies prove that 20 minutes of nature connection per day is beneficial both for mental and physical health. Slow down. Remind yourself that there's nothing to do. Give yourself the time to experience the moment. It is time to be, not do. Sitting or moving slowly is okay. There is a difference between crossing off the to-do list in your garden or pushing the body to work out and relaxing to be and connect with life around you. Allow your body and mind to be.

2) Allow yourself to be immersed in the experience and if you are sensing into the moment, you can take photographs or videos of what you see and take in the beauty of the moment with you. This creative process is a way for you to reconnect with yourself and your expression. Your photos will reflect what you are sensing, even if you are not a photographer.

It is a refreshing self-reflection exercise to sort through these images later, when you are at home or at work. You can use these images as screensavers and phone backgrounds. The beauty of the moment can be used to breathe life into the more difficult or blah moments ahead. You can share them with people and spread joy.

Take a few minutes and learn the basics in how to use the camera on your phone. Knowing how to best focus on an object will make things a lot more fun. My skills in photography have improved so much over the years of nature connecting that I now have a business selling my images on wall art and greeting cards. You never know where your passions will take you!

3)  Take notes or record a memo if any good ideas pop up along the way.

4)  Plant ID - with an iPhone you can take a photo of a plant and use it to ID plants and animals that you encounter. It's not perfect, and you will want to further confirm the identification when you are at home.

## Next Up... MAKING YOUR WAY BACK TO YOUR LIFE....

The last three steps are the benefits of nature connection in use in real life.

# Chapter Twelve

## Step Five

### LIVE with courage.

Courage is a virtue where you voluntarily face personal risk in pursuit of a worthy goal. It is a human strength and in that, it can be built like a muscle. You build courage by being courageous. Your emotional state, social influences and values all affect your ability to be courageous.

Psychological courage is the strength that allows you to overcome personal limitations to live a more authentic life. It increases your chances for personal evolution to become your best self. It involves being vulnerable and having the confidence to take risks to go for your dreams.

You need courage if you are going to act with integrity.

You need courage to be brave in the face of opposition.

You need courage to follow through with enough persistence and emotional regulation to accomplish the things you set out to do.

You need courage if you are someone who vitally invested in living your best life.

Part of psychological courage is being able to be honest about who you are and accept yourself. It's about taking ownership for your actions. Greenspaces provide the perfect environment for self-reflection and to offer self-acceptance.

From a place of calm and stillness in nature, your intuition will be clearer. Creativity and problem solving is stronger.

Ask yourself, did I gain any insights about myself or my life during my nature connection today? Then ask yourself: what is my next step? Write it down, sketch it out, journal, paint, or dream about where you want to go with this. After you answer the questions, take a courageous step, either big or small, in that direction. When you ask these questions often, and act on them, even if they are small steps, not only will you develop your strength in courage, but you will also evolve and grow. Clarity will come in each step you take. Small courageous shifts for the better create the possibility for big changes in the long run.

Looking back, one day you will see how nature connection and taking time for yourself have been some of the best moves to propel your life forward in amazing ways.

## Miss Angel Archetype

Miss Angel is never one to dive in headfirst. She hates diving headfirst. She has dreams where she is flying, and dreams of swimming deep underwater, but less dreams where she is diving.

She feels like an outsider, but she's not sure why. She knows there is more, but she's not sure how to get there.

She grows up in a small town with small ambitions for girls. Where she's from, the girls watch sports and the guys play sports, namely hockey. Same with music, guys play music. The girls are not encouraged to have the same ambition or freedom as boys. Girls are encouraged to be nice, to get along. They stuff down their tough emotions, such as anger. They never want to look like they are being negative. They seem obsessed with finding love. They don't believe they can be happy by themselves. The girls in this town do all they can to be perfect. They are always talking about the latest styles and follow trends to a T. It seems like the biggest concern of every girl is how they look. They feel like they need to wear makeup all the time. It is such a weird and limiting scene, it might be hard to believe that such a place exists.

Miss Angel visits her grandma at her tiny home surrounded by trees and a big garden. They have long talks. Her grandma has lived a long life and at the right time, she delivers the best advice. One day Miss Angel is worrying about her bleak future. She doesn't want to settle down with the boring life offered in her town. Her grandma replies, "You can do anything you put your mind to."

"Grandma, you just said ANYTHING."

Grandma replies, "Why not?"

Miss Angel scoffs at first, imagining the scene where everyone did what they put their minds to doing. That would never happen in her town! The idea makes her laugh, and it gets her thinking a bit. Shortly after that, she wonders what would she do if she allowed herself to do what she wanted to do.

Emotions can run high during adolescence. When she needs a break from it all, she takes long walks down country roads under the big Albertan skies. She listens to the wind, she looks at the trees and plants, she pulls blades of grass and feels the rough texture in her hands. She prays for solutions to her problems, she dreams big, and in the process, she gains clarity about herself. She has revelations about her life, and she lets her emotions out. She feels her feelings. Being surrounded by nature reminds her of the goodness surrounding her, it reminds her of possibility. It gives her a sense of faith in herself. She knows her life is worth more than what she can find in her town.

It's not like she exists in a bubble. She knows that there are places outside of her town where women have no limitations. She decides she wants to move there as soon as she can.

She does her research and applies for a scholarship to go to university in Vancouver. Much to her surprise, she's accepted with a full scholarship. Not only that, but she meets a few people from her town who are actually not so closed minded. Where were you guys?

For the first time ever, she dives headfirst in a new direction. She moves to the west coast. When she arrives in Vancouver, she's a little overwhelmed with all the things she needs to do to set up for school and in residence. She feels closed off and unsure if she made the right decision.

One of the first days in university, she's totally lost and late for class. She meets a super approachable woman with a big smile who gives her directions. She meets her again, by chance, after class. She introduces her to more people, and after that, her world expands a great deal more. These new friends are much different than the folks back home. They are not afraid to be themselves. These new friends are unique, expressive, and fun to be around. It's very refreshing.

She's in constant motion in this city. She experiments with new styles and decides that she doesn't like the same styles she wore back home. She's found a look that suits her more. She's studying all she can and decides to focus on architecture. She takes in indie music and movies on the weekend, sometimes with friends, and sometimes on her own. She makes a few mistakes in life and love but bounces back. She visits the market, tries new foods. Each week she takes time to visit the beach and the parks in the city. While in nature, she takes time to consider her goals, and to make sure she is on track. She explores her emotional terrain and allows herself to feel her emotions. This practice is such a big part of her success.

She loves life in this city. There's room to breathe. She can be all she wants to be. Thinking of her grandma's advice, maybe it's not so crazy to chase her dreams. She transforms from Miss Angel to the Aligned Architect.

# Chapter Thirteen

## Step Six

### AWARENESS - of ourselves in our world.

The regular practice of tuning into nature makes you better able to tune into the actions and intentions of those around you. It helps you develop the habit of tuning into your intuition and feeling your feelings. This is priceless.

One example of where this is of benefit, is being able to pay attention to who brings your energy up and to who pulls you down. It's a great idea to spend 80% of your time with people who lift you up. Spend time with people who lift you up, make you feel at peace, and bring out the best in you.

Tuning into your intuition also helps with noticing when

people say one thing and do another. When you recognize it, you can choose to do something about it, like addressing it or walking away from it.

Since the Stellar method was created for people who tend to lose themselves in their personal relationships, exhibiting codependency, it's a good idea to delve into the topic of codependency versus interdependent relationships. As you will see below, an awareness of who you are is key in creating and maintaining healthy relationships. Fortunately, the Stellar method for nature connection is a regular habit supporting a strong relationship with yourself. It is a great way to offer self-care.

Codependency results when a person doesn't have a rock-solid sense of who they are and they look to something outside of themselves, either another person, or sometimes a substance or an activity, to define them. In relationships, there tends to be limited freedom, and growth. Codependent people rely on their partner to meet their emotional needs. They feel quite distressed, burdened with guilt or shame, when their relationship is not going well. Codependent relationships perpetuate the problem in someone not knowing themselves. They rely so heavily on outside sources to define them that it is almost impossible for someone to be themselves while in a codependent relationship.

Simply put, a codependent person is enmeshed with their partner. They are focused on others and lose themselves in their relationships. They can either be busily involved in meeting the needs of their partner or they might demand that their partner meet all their needs. It is not a fun relationship. Since there is little freedom, people in these relationships might feel the need to ask permission from their partner to go out with others. They might worry way more about how to make their partner happy, than making themselves happy. They might blame their partner if they feel sad, angry, or dissatisfied in any way and expect their partner to soothe their emotions. They might be scared to voice their opinion before hearing what their partner thinks. They might spend every spare second with their partner because they can't stand being apart.

It can show up as a bad mix of no boundaries, and people pleasing behavior. There can be poor communication, blame games, and emotional reactivity. There can be a tendency for codependent people to manipulate and control their partner. This low fun relationship continues with difficulty in emotional intimacy and low self-esteem. To top it off, there are very few personal interests or goals outside the relationship.

## Wouldn't you prefer to be more of yourself, shine like a star, and feel great in your personal relationships?

A healthy star shines bright no matter where they go. They have their own constellations of friends, families, interests, values, hobbies, and opinions. They are stars all on their own, they are not here to prop up another star or borrow light from another star. They don't wish they were a different star. They know who they are and they are beautifully unique stars all on their own. They don't seek out the opinions of others to feel more like a star. It doesn't work that way.

When two bright stars, totally secure in their own starriness, come together, they can form a vividly beautiful mini constellation. They are not together to avoid loneliness, they come together because they enjoy being together. They are secure in their own starriness, and they support each other emotionally in their own little haven constellation. Neither of them needs to seek validation that they are shining. They are not afraid to be who they are, they are not afraid to say no. They can shine in their own way without worrying that it will break up their constellation. They would never consider dimming for their star partner. They don't lose their essence to be in this constellation, they continue to be their own little stars. They are interdependent stars.

Interdependent relationships are made of a magic that can only be found when both partners have a clear understanding of who they are. Each person has a strong sense of self. They know what they like and what they value. This isn't a union brought together through desperation and loneliness. They are each secure in who they are and they express themselves openly and authentically.

People in interdependent relationships carve out time to prioritize themselves in self-care and individual interests. They take care of their physical health by exercising, relaxing and eating healthy foods they enjoy. Each of them manages their emotions in healthy ways. They each take responsibility for their behaviors. They are mindful and take the time to care for their own emotional terrains, ensuring that they feel their best for themselves and for dynamic growth to the relationship. When they get together, they retain their own interests, hobbies and social circles. Neither of them needs to play small to be together.

They find security, trust, and reliability in their relationship. Communication is strong, clear, and reflects respect. It is safe to express needs and desires. Active listening, free of judgment and criticism, reflects empathy towards one another. Each maintains strong boundaries.

This isn't a relationship where two halves make a whole. This is a relational alchemy where two complete people come together and create even more through the inherent freedom for continual growth and transformation.

Together they create a haven of emotional support to weather life's storms. They trust they can be vulnerable with each other without fear that this will end the relationship. They maintain their own individuality within the relationship, and this allows for sustainable, genuine and meaningful physical and emotional connections without fear of losing themselves or being manipulated.

To function well within an interdependent relationship, especially if you have a history of codependency, you need to support yourself and remain aware of who you are individually and in your relationships. Time away in nature allows you to prioritize yourself, reflect, and to stay in touch with who you are and how you are feeling on a regular basis. The Stellar method for nature connection helps you maintain that strong sense of self so that no matter what, whether you are in a relationship or not, you are functioning at your best. You are your most successful, autonomous, and authentic self in all areas of your life.

## Stray Sister Archetype

The Stray Sister starts out left out. This archetype is on the outside and wants nothing more than to fit in. She's willing to do what it takes to hold onto her job and all the great friends she has made at work. She strives to add value everywhere she goes.

Always happy to help, she gets sucked into other people's projects. She wants to do good, so she doesn't mind. Co-workers tend to dump their work on her. On Monday morning, a work colleague asks her to write their report for them and draft a couple emails. She might have to skip lunch, but it's no problem. In the afternoon, she's designing a few trainings, and a coworker walks into her office, states she's feeling sick, and asks her to administer a consultation. She'll have to stay late, but sure!

Tuesday morning, she is working with a coworker designing more training modules. In the afternoon when they present the training to their team, her co-worker takes all the credit for her best ideas. Ouch!

Wednesday, she has meetings all day, another co-worker decides it's sunny and he wants to golf. He asks her if she will share her notes from the afternoon meetings. Sure, have a great game!

On Thursday she notices that the people she's helping seem to have more time for fun. At first, she's curious and asks why, but there is no clear answer, so she continues. Fawning, she's never going to be so bold as to rock the boat.

She's got a ton of work complete before the weekend, but on Friday morning she spends an hour consoling and trying to fix the crying coworker with a love life drama.

On Friday afternoon, everyone left the office early but she's still at it. The work for others never really seems to end, and in fact the piles seem to be accumulating. Attempting to justify her situation, she reasons to herself that she's become quite adept at all of these tasks. Let's face it, by now she's the only one who can do what she does. She smiles for a second, then frowns. She feels used and resentful. She powers through the rest of the work and hates herself for doing it.

Over the weekend, she makes herself an espresso and takes a moment to reflect. She would love to have a pet, maybe a cat, or a dog. Ah, forget it. A pet would be crazy, her workdays are way too long. After that, she wonders when she last made time to visit her favourite market. It's been years! When did she last visit her friends? She texts one out of the blue and there's no response. She looks in the mirror and wow, she notices she looks so disheveled. She hasn't even made time for a haircut in months. She feels sad and ends up depressed. She grabs the Ben & Jerry's and decides to spend the day watching Downton Abbey for the 5th time.

Sunday morning, she wakes up, and she realizes she doesn't

recognize herself anymore. She puts on her boots, her whole body feels heavy, each movement is so difficult as she puts on her coat.

As she walks to the forest, the feelings come out. She starts to cry. And this surprised her. She didn't know she was so sad. At first, she simply feels her feelings. Then, she looks around and notices so many beautiful aspects of the environment. The sun is shining with a perfect warm glow. A beetle moving across the path, birds chirping and flitting about. It makes her see her life in the context of now, within the context of this beautiful planet. It reminds her of possibility. Spending time in the forest feels good. She challenges herself to go each day after work and each day the emotions come out. She relaxes as she walks through the forest, she sees beautiful trees, sunsets and forest animals. The forest is welcoming. It mirrors life within her. She always feels better when she returns home.

The daily practice of sensing helps her find herself, her center. It helps her pay attention to her feelings throughout the day. It gives her a craving for more in her life: more freedom, more peace, and more time for what she is here to do. She decides to look for work elsewhere, and she finds a new job right away. Adjusting to her new work is a steep learning curve for the first few weeks, but after that, she's good. She is determined to maintain clear boundaries at this new workplace. It wasn't so hard, people at her new workplace are much better at their jobs. Everything has changed and it's a good thing. Her hair is freshly cut and styled, she purchases new clothes for a new look. She feels great. She then decides to check out the animal shelter. An adorable little orange fluffy cat stares at her sweetly and grabs her heart. She adopts her and names her Maizy.

When Stray Sister takes the time to look at her life and decide she wants more, and she commits to doing all she can to feel better, the parts of her life that were not in alignment with her new energy fell apart. When they did, a whole new world opened. A whole new world that reflected her authentically. One that respected her contributions and boundaries. She's happier and feels a great satisfaction knowing she's living a life that's hers to create. Committing to daily self-care allowed a more expanded concept of herself transforming the Stray Sister to the glowing Fabulous Feminine.

# Chapter Fourteen

## Step Seven

### REMAIN OPEN - Wait, there's more.  Remaining open after facing life's challenges.

Step Seven is to REMAIN OPEN.  Life offers many challenges.  Change is inevitable.  Allow the practice of nature connection to keep you open to new and exciting chapters waiting to unfold in your life.

One of the biggest messages I have received through the daily practice of nature connection is the way we cycle in and out of seasons.  Nothing stays the same.  We make our way to the heart of each season, but it is more of a dance than walking in a straight line.  There may be a bad stretch of intensely hot or cold or wet or dry weather, but it ends, eventually. The intense moments of life all have an ending. The devastating grief you feel after the death of a loved one or divorce, or any loss, will not be here forever. And it may not end overnight, but they will eventually end. You may start to feel a little better each day and then be hit with grief again like a spring snowstorm. Nothing ever stays the same. Each day is new. Each season, a little different. It's impossible to let yourself get caught in being all bitter about the cold of winter when you suddenly feel the reprieve of spring. Similarly, allow yourself to move through and move on and embrace each season of your life.

Commit to self-care, keep your heart open to goodness in you, and create big change in your life.

## Know Nothing Maiden Archetype

The last archetype to visit is the Know Nothing Maiden. She has a hunch there is more to explore, so she sets out on a quest for knowledge. Those with authority seem like a good choice for the best knowledge. She signs up to attend an institution qualified to offer certified knowledge. They are the ones who catalog the most important information. So, off she goes, doing all she can to gain valuable knowledge.

While there, she notices that some were better at retaining knowledge than others. She's okay at comprehending new concepts, but sometimes it feels unattainable. It was the kind of knowledge that seems to require new muscles. This must mean it's the most valuable. She catches a whiff of the fact that there are different types of knowledge, but she only wants the best, so she decides to not explore the others, and sticks with the one. She speaks with people in the institution, and they affirm her decision. Their response is usually a segue to more concepts. So, she continues, doing an okay job grasping what seems so elusive, and spending plenty of time nodding as she listens to those around her elucidate their vast amounts of knowledge.

She ends up feeling more and more exclusive. It starts with thinking there are those who know, and all the others, the sheep. There are so many hilarious stories about those who don't know. Did you know there's an idiot tax for the sheep? They pay more because they don't know better.

She's obsessed with this knowledge; she is more and more concerned that she's precise. She begins to distrust her own thoughts, her own way of expressing herself. She continuously seeks knowledge from outside sources. This is such an extreme sport, only the elite can keep up. It's a mad chase. I mean, will she ever have enough? Does she even know how to write a sentence?

Amid the mustering, she one day has a conversation with someone in the know. A philosopher in women's studies. In her gentle way, she beckons the Know Nothing Maiden back to what she calls the greatest task: Know Thyself. What does that mean? Exactly what you think, know who you are. This is a striking conversation, somehow it rings true, enough so that it causes the Know Nothing Maiden to return to this idea many times over many years.

Eventually, someone Harvard educated coaxes her to consider that the vastest resource of knowledge resides in our innate knowledge, our intuition. To access the truth, the most accurate filter is not an institution or another expert, it is through the brain, the gut, and the heart. For so many years she lost herself in pursuit of the greatest, when the best was ready and waiting for the taking. It was from her and didn't require validation from great people or institutions. The Know Nothing Maiden begins to hone her skills in accessing her inner knowing and in doing so transforms into the Wise Witch.

Bring new energy,
lighten up,
allow space to relax,
recalibrate,
and prioritize yourself.

# Chapter Fifteen

## To the stars
## with STELLAR Nature Connection

Over the last number of years, you have likely noticed the dawning of a new age. This new age has your face lit, your eyes hungry for more, your brain and body fully engaged and consuming a light emitted from screens of all shapes and sizes, readily available around the clock. Each time you face another screen you are consuming the light, meaning the ideas, the humour, the opinions, the sales pitches, the entertainment, news, and more, always more. You may be open to receive so much of this light, but is it too much? Is your relationship with this light lopsided? Could this relationship be healthier? Could you shine more?

The book was written to help people with a tendency to over-give and lose themselves in relationships, including technology and social media. You may not be able to pinpoint the origin of these tendencies, all you really know is the now. Nature connection is an accessible practice that supports you in staying true to your authentic self. Practices like these are especially important if you have a history of codependency, attracting relationships with narcissists and other self-interested people. It is also helpful for you if you struggle with your relationship to social media and technology. This practice involves feeling your feelings, tuning into your surroundings, grounding, gratitude, listening to your intuition, and raising your vibe. All of this brings you back to a deeper understanding of who you are. This practice not only gives you tools for your daily life, but it also supports you as you work towards achieving your goals. Alignment on all levels is easier when you take the time to care for yourself, your bodies and emotions. When you have the courage to prioritize yourself, when you choose to play the star of your life, the Universe sits up and takes notice, offering major positive shifts to support you.

Spending 120 minutes a week in nature is necessary for mental and physical health. For this reason, time in nature is never a waste of time. Taking it further, nature connection supports you in making the most of your time in nature and helps you to shine like the bright star that you are in your own life. When major upheavals happen in your life, you can find support through nature connection. As you encounter day to day challenges, you know you have a daily practice of nature connection to help you face it all with a higher vibration, with strength, and from a place of peace.

Like the leaves in the fall, you begin the Stellar method of nature connection by shedding some of that which would otherwise hold us back from new seasons and opportunities in our future. You feel your feelings, name what is happening, and decide what we really want. You write the story of your life, and you get to choose what you want today. You allow yourself to shed old energies, forgive, and act from a higher vibration.

From this higher vibration you cultivate more of what you want in your life by offering gratitude for the goodness already in your life and in your environment. You ground yourself and move ahead with a calm and centered energy. You set aside your worries about things beyond your control, practice staying grounded in the present moment and trust that you are connected to Source.

Refreshed, grateful and grounded, you set out with curiosity and explore aspects of yourself and your environment. You follow your senses and sense anew, to experience awe, and to take in beauty. In this, nature consciousness develops to offer connection to the more-than-human-world and to the self, within the context of your planet. You foster healthy relationships with the-more-than-human-world and the planet. You explore and remain curious about yourself and the world around you. Feeling a connection to all life is key in developing a profound love of self.

From here, you are primed for the best messages to bubble up from within or to arise from unusual and new experiences in nature. Your intuition is heightened in this relaxing yet dynamic space. You can't force it or control it, but be ready, because there is a good chance you will receive a message through sight, sound, a deep knowing or feeling. Nature reflects truth through signs and symbols. This practice strengthens your instincts and the practice of listening to your intuition.

This practice makes you stronger and able to live authentically, from a higher vibration, igniting creativity to enhance all aspects of your life, from problem solving to having fun. It also helps us trust your intuition when we are interacting with others. You practice paying attention to both words and actions of the people in your life. You foster a new awareness of who you are. The practice of letting go a little each day helps you remain open to new relationships and opportunities, even after facing life's challenges.

When you take the time to nature connect, do you notice any shifts in your body and in your life? Do you learn anything new about yourself? Your surroundings? The seasons? Your city? Are you noticing more in nature or the more-than-human-world?

This book is only the beginning. You and your practice of nature connection will continue to evolve as you grow. My hope is that you will continue to explore new avenues in your knowledge of self, your emotions, and your life. If you would like a free Stellar Nature Connection Guide visit https://mailchi.mp/dailynatureconnection/w9ka9vb8z1

Or visit my website fleurbain.com for more resources supporting you in your quest for self-love through nature connection.

This is change, baby, and you were meant to evolve.
It is possible to create goodness once again, after tough times.
It is possible to shine even brighter each day, like the star you are.
The star you were destined to be.

# Sources

Andersen, Liisa et al. Nature Exposure and Its Effects on Immune System Functioning: A Systematic Review. https://www.ncbi.nlm.nih.gov/pmc/articles/PMC7913501/

Beck, Martha Nibley Steering by starlight: find your right life, no matter what!
New York, Rodale, 2008.

Beyer, Catherine. The 5 Elemental Symbols: Fire, Water, Air, Earth, and Spirit. https://www.learnreligions.com/elemental-symbols-4122788

Brown, Joshua & Joel Wong. How Gratitude Changes Your

and Your Brain. https://greatergood.berkeley.edu/article/item/how_gratitude_changes_you_and_your_brain

Bubnis, Daniel. 8 Health Benefits of Getting Back to Nature and Spending Time Outside https://www.healthline.com/health/health-benefits-of-being-outdoors#reduced-depression

Burn, Shawn M. Are Women More Codependent Than Men? https://www.psychologytoday.com/us/blog/presence-mind/201709/are-women-more-codependent-men

Clarke, Jodi. How to Build a Relationship Based on Interdependence. https://www.verywellmind.com/how-to-build-a-relationship-based-on-interdependence-4161249

Dale, Cyndi. (2022) Energy Healing Certification Part 1 - The Immersion Unit Two, Class 3: The Subtle Elements Underlying All of Your Existence & Ways to Use Them for Grounding, Healing & Creating the Life You Desire. The Shift Network.

Davies, Nikki. How to build your psychological courage. https://www.wellbeing.com.au/mind-spirit/mind/how-to-build-your-courage.html

Dean, Ben. Defining Courage. https://www.authentichappiness.sas.upenn.edu/newsletters/authentichappinesscoaching/courage

Diotaiuti, Pierluigi et al. Internet addiction in young adults: The role of impulsivity and codependency. https://

www.frontiersin.org/journals/psychiatry/articles/10.3389/fp-syt.2022.893861/full

García de Jalón, Silvestre et al. The influence of urban greens-paces on people's physical activity: A population based study in Spain. https://www.sciencedirect.com/science/article/abs/pii/S0169204621001924

Greener streets linked to better sleep. https://www.science-daily.com/releases/2024/03/240325114155.htm#

Hall, Katherine. Mothers' accounts of the impact of being in nature on postnatal wellbeing: a focus group study. https://www.ncbi.nlm.nih.gov/pmc/articles/PMC9869311/

Harding, Stephan. What Does It Mean to be Human? https://humansandnature.org/to-be-human-stephan-harding/

Hawkins, David R. The Map of Consciousness Explained. Carlsbad, Hay House, 2020.

Heid, Markham. You Asked: Is It Bad to Be Inside All Day? https://time.com/collection/guide-to-happiness/4306455/stress-relief-nature/#

Heshmat, Shahram. 10 Sources of a Courageous Mind-set. https://www.psychologytoday.com/us/blog/sci-ence-choice/202207/10-sources-courageous-mindset

How Indoor Environments Affect People's Lives: 10 things

you need to know. https://www.terramai.com/blog/10-ways-indoor-environments-affect-people/

I Had To Lose You To Love Me: 3 Steps to Overcoming Codependency https://embracingyoutherapy.com/i-had-to-lose-you-to-love-me-3-steps-to-overcoming-codependency/

Indoor Air Quality: What are the trends in indoor air quality and their effects on human health? https://www.epa.gov/report-environment/indoor-air-quality

It's official – spending time outside is good for you. https://www.sciencedaily.com/releases/2018/07/180706102842.htm

Jimenez, Marcia P. et al. Associations between Nature Exposure and Health: A Review of Evidence. https://www.ncbi.nlm.nih.gov/pmc/articles/PMC8125471/

Jo, Hyunju et al. Physiological Benefits of Viewing Nature: A Systematic Review of Indoor Experiments. https://www.ncbi.nlm.nih.gov/pmc/articles/PMC6926748/

Jung, Carl. Memories, Dreams, And Reflections. New York City, Vintage Books, 1989. Pages 225-226.

Keniger, Lucy E. et al. What are the Benefits of Interacting with Nature? https://www.ncbi.nlm.nih.gov/pmc/articles/PMC3709294/

Kim, John. Nurturing Secure Attachment: Building Healthy

Relationships. https://www.psychologytoday.com/us/blog/the-angry-therapist/202307/nurturing-secure-attachment-building-healthy-relationships

Linn, Denise. Energy Strands: The Ultimate Guide to Clearing the Cords That Are Constricting Your Life. Carlsbad, Hay House, 2018.

Luo, Elaine K. The Effect of Negative Ions. https://www.healthline.com/health/negative-ions.

Muñoz, Alicia. How Do You Overcome Codependency? A Therapist's Guide. https://www.mindbodygreen.com/articles/how-to-stop-being-codependent

Nature walk enhances certain executive control processes in the brain. https://www.news-medical.net/news/20240130/Nature-walk-enhances-certain-executive-control-processes-in-the-brain.aspx

Nguygen, Jessica & Eric Brymer. Nature-Based Guided Imagery as an Intervention for State Anxiety. https://www.ncbi.nlm.nih.gov/pmc/articles/PMC6176042/

Nichols, Bethany. Plants Have Feelings Too. https://www.bbcearth.com/news/plants-have-feelings-too

Orloff, Judith. How To Develop Intuition. https://drjudith-orloff.com/how-to-develop-intuition/

Pearson, David G. & Tony Craig. The great outdoors? Exploring the mental health benefits of natural environments. https://www.ncbi.nlm.nih.gov/pmc/articles/PMC4204431/

Pedersen, Traci. 7 Examples of Common Codependent Behaviors https://psychcentral.com/health/signs-of-codependence-codependent-behavior

RAS (Reticular Activating System) https://extension.umn.edu/two-you-video-series/ras

Robbins, Jim. Ecopsychology: How Immersion in Nature Benefits Your Health. https://e360.yale.edu/features/ecopsychology-how-immersion-in-nature-benefits-your-health

Rook, Graham A. Regulation of the immune system by biodiversity from the natural environment: An ecosystem service essential to health. https://www.ncbi.nlm.nih.gov/pmc/articles/PMC3831972/

Roy Chowdhury, Madhuleena. The Neuroscience of Gratitude and Effects on the Brain. https://positivepsychology.com/neuroscience-of-gratitude/

Rubik, Beverly et al. Biofield Science and Healing: History, Terminology, and Concepts. https://www.ncbi.nlm.nih.gov/pmc/articles/PMC4654789/

Ryan, Richard M. et al. Vitalizing effects of being outdoors and in nature. https://www.sciencedirect.com/science/article/abs/pii/S0272494409000838

Salutogenesis. https://en.wikipedia.org/wiki/Salutogenesis

Sanderson, Catherine. A Simple Strategy for Boosting Happiness and Health: Spend Time in Nature. https://medium.com/@casanderson/a-simple-strategy-for-boosting-happiness-and-health-spend-time-in-nature-e5c52aeb2646

Sauber Millacci, Tiffany. What is Gratitude and Why Is It So Important? https://positivepsychology.com/gratitude-appreciation

Seasonal affective disorder, winter blues and self-care tips to get ahead or symptoms. https://health.ucdavis.edu/blog/cultivating-health/seasonal-affective-disorder-winter-blues-and-self-care-tips-to-get-ahead-of-symptoms/2023/11

Shepley, Mardelle. The Impact of Green Space on Violent Crime in Urban Environments: An Evidence Synthesis. https://www.ncbi.nlm.nih.gov/pmc/articles/PMC6950486/

Smith, Kurt. Codependency vs. Interdependency. https://psychcentral.com/lib/codependency-vs-interdependency

Study linking beneficial bacteria to mental health makes top 10 list for brain research. https://www.colorado.edu/today/2017/01/05/study-linking-beneficial-bacteria-mental-health-makes-top-10-list-brain-research

Tanasugarn, Annie. Creating Healthy Interdependence in

Your Relationship. https://www.psychologytoday.com/us/blog/understanding-ptsd/202210/creating-healthy-interdependence-in-your-relationship

Thai, Linda (2024, January 11th) A Conversation with Linda Thai on the topic of Rethinking Attachment; Towards Relational Wholeness. A community gathering organized by SAND

3 ways getting outside into nature helps improve your health. https://health.ucdavis.edu/blog/cultivating-health/3-ways-getting-outside-into-nature-helps-improve-your-health/2023/05

Travers, Mark. 3 Ways To Transform A Codependency Cycle Into a Healthy Relationship. https://www.forbes.com/sites/traversmark/2022/11/09/3-ways-to-transform-a-codependency-cycle-into-a-healthy-relationship/

Ulrich, R. S. View through a window may influence recovery from surgery. https://pubmed.ncbi.nlm.nih.gov/6143402/

Using Trees and Vegetation to Reduce Heat Islands. https://www.epa.gov/heatislands/using-trees-and-vegetation-reduce-heat-islands

Videle, Jimmy. The Sentience of Plants: Could plants be sentient? https://humaneherald.org/2018/02/06/the-sentience-of-plants/

What Is Mindfulness? https://greatergood.berkeley.edu/topic/mindfulness/definition#what-is-mindfulness

White, Matthew P. et al. Spending at least 120 minutes a week in nature is associated with good health and wellbeing. https://www.nature.com/articles/s41598-019-44097-3

Weir, Kirsten. Nurtured by nature: Psychological research is advancing our understanding of how time in nature can improve our mental health and sharpen our cognition. https://www.apa.org/monitor/2020/04/nurtured-nature

Wolf, Lukas J. et al. Is Variety the Spice of Life? An Experimental Investigation into the Effects of Species Richness on Self-Reported Mental Well-Being. https://journals.plos.org/plosone/article?id=10.1371/journal.pone.0170225

Writer, Simone. Nope. You're NOT codependent. https://simonewriter.com/nope-youre-not-codependent/

Yan, Xiujing et al. Spatial analysis of the ecological effects of negative air ions in urban vegetated areas: A case study in Maiji, China. https://www.sciencedirect.com/science/article/abs/pii/S1618866715000928

Your Brain Needs Fractals, So Go Outside. https://www.syfy.com/syfy-wire/fractals-in-nature-need-to-be-seen-by-human-brain

# Acknowledgements

I offer my sincere thanks to everyone who supported me during my time of sweet solitude as I worked through my stuff and wrote this book.

Thanks to friends, especially Jennifer Epp, and to my family, including my grandfather, parents, uncle, brothers, nieces and nephews for phone calls, check-ins, and encouragement. Thanks to my kind and thoughtful neighbours Jim and Tina.

Special thanks to my life coach Karen Strang Allen and to the readers of this book, including Ginger Lily, Sarka Halas, and Deborah Ostrovsky.

# Meet the Author

Tammy Schmidt is the creativity behind Fleurbain and Daily Nature Connection. She is a clinically trained herbalist & certified nature and forest therapy guide who helps people improve their mental and physical health by deepening their connections to the natural world. She works as an experiential herbalist, guiding people through first-hand experiences with plants and trees. Tamara is called to work with people experiencing a nature deficit, helping them find nature connections. Strong relationships with the more-than-human-world have a ripple effect benefiting all beings.

In this book, Stellar, she illustrates how nature connection fosters self-love, especially for people with a tendency to over-give.

www.ingramcontent.com/pod-product-compliance
Lightning Source LLC
Chambersburg PA
CBHW030838090426
42737CB00009B/1015
*9781068940200*